THE UNIVERSAL SISTERHOOD

Monika Wilbanks

THE UNIVERSAL SISTERHOOD

And Women Shall Lead

TATE PUBLISHING & *Enterprises*

Published by Tate Publishing & Enterprises, LLC
127 E. Trade Center Terrace | Mustang, Oklahoma 73064 USA
1.888.361.9473 | www.tatepublishing.com

Tate Publishing is committed to excellence in the publishing industry. The company reflects the philosophy established by the founders, based on Psalm 68:11,
"The Lord gave the word and great was the company of those who published it."

Interior design by Joel Uber

Published in the United States of America

ISBN: 978-1-61739-942-8
1. Religion; Christian Life, Women's Issues
2. Body, Mind & Spirit; Spirituality, General
11.03.28

References to man—"he," "him," etc.—may be gender neutral and pertain to all of humankind, both women and men.

God, the Holy Spirit, the Holy Father, the Holy Trinity are referred to as male, even though He/She has female and male aspects.

Child of the Universe

You came from above and you will return
To your rightful place.
You have shared a planet and a moment with me.
You have taken the wisdom given to you
And used it for the growth of your soul.
Well done, my friend.
M. K. Wilbanks

Dedication

This book is dedicated to the Supreme Being in our midst.

He is recognized as the Spirit of Truth, Power, and Wisdom, through which all things are created. He is the life of our spirit, the substance of our soul, and the intelligence of our thoughts. He is the beginning and the end.

He has brought the kingdom of God to earth. Principalities and powers in high places have become null and void. In this era of the Holy Spirit, all powers must bow to Him. The Ancient of Days said, "Behold, I make all things new." For this reason, the old must give way to the new. The only power that now reigns is the Most High God.

Thank you, Father.

To my beloved Aubree, who decided to be born into this family as a female. Her generation will put the words of this book into practice. As she becomes a woman, this book will be a light on her path and to all the women in her time. She will not give her power to anyone.

Table of Contents

Universal Sisterhood

Watch out world, here we come
walking through the door.
Leaving pain, leaving shame,
we now have the floor.

Giving wings to someone else
is no more our gain.
Ever going, ever growing,
steadfast we remain.

I am woman, hear me well,
stand aside and listen.
I have something great to say,
for we have all arisen.

Universal sisterhood,
a rolling river of love.
We come to banish violence and war
and carry the sign of the dove.

M.K.Wilbanks

Foreword

A Message from My Spiritual Mother

My spiritual mother and beloved sister in Christ, Beverly Marts, is contributing this message, which the Spirit gave her to address the issue of universal sisterhood:

We might ponder here what "universal" conveys to us. What message does it give us? The word says to us—shared purpose, all-inclusive, many facets, singing a song (verse) together. The power of this song comes with the ability and inclusiveness to move from the abstract to the practical application. Only this will bring the result we want—things hoped for and long desired. Changes will come that will impact our daily lives and enable us to interact with one another in peace and unity. The true message of this age of Spirit (Holy Spirit) is that we are now in oneness. In the age of Spirit, there are neither male nor female, neither young nor old, neither black nor white; truly we are one. This is the age when heaven and earth merge as one life, one reality, one rule and love; this is the tie that binds. Did we not ask for this in the LORD's Prayer when we said, "thy will be done on earth as it is in heaven"? Since all creation was created in love, we must go back to that first love we shared with our Creator in the beginning that first love which we did not compromise, equivocate, or question. Love is always the same yesterday, today, and tomorrow. It always answers to the one life that was ours and will be ours forever. Are we not eternal beings? Of course we are—our God is eternal.

Therefore, we share this with Him. In this wonderful age of Spirit, man and woman must come into full realization of his or her divine self. The practical manifestation of this in our mundane world brings wonders and changes. Our universal sisterhood must be at the forefront of those changes, for we have been given the nurturing spirit that is necessary to sustain any lasting change. Without nurturing, can there be any growth? To nurture means to take care of, to shelter, to protect, to comfort. It is that umbrella of love that only women can provide. This universal sisterhood has moved from a position of weakness to a position of strength, from tragedy to triumph. Have there been pitfalls along the way? Of course! The drama of two steps forward and one step back.

Physically, we have been liberated. But at the right time, we will now experience the spiritual liberation as well. One is not complete without the other. It will be all in God's time. Our ultimate goal and inevitable triumph was destined from the beginning. Within the mind of our loving Father, we were always victors, never victims. The journey itself has taught us this remarkable lesson and gave us strength for this time. Strength always comes through adversity, until we learn that strength was given to us from the beginning. Once we know this, adversity vanishes from the drama of this life. Bondage of any kind brings reaction in the flesh, but action in the spirit. Spirit is the plane of cause. Our mundane world is the plane of effect.

The battle always exists in the mind. As we express in real terms what many call the mind of Christ, or the super conscious mind, we are merely marching with our true self—that which we were at the beginning (our garden of Eden), which has always been waiting for us. For in truth, we are wondrously made. Peace, love, joy, prosperity, and perfect health belong irrevocably to us by divine right, and once we truly understand this truth, these attributes will manifest in us.

The question arises, "What is the spiritual age and how do we receive the true message of the spiritual age?" The spiritual age started with the new millennium. It brought us into the era of the Holy Spirit. As we have gone through the physical and mental ages, we now approach the age of Spirit. We now want to know more about our souls. Our souls waited a long time for this. The true message must be found in our hearts; we must experience the modern-day Passover. What is this? Let us refer to the Bible passage in Matthew 3:11, which speaks of the baptism of fire, which cleanses us of all sins. Is this enough? After this baptism, we can hear the voice and practice the true teaching.

Who is our true teacher? That voice within us is the Spirit (Holy Spirit) incarnate. He has released His gospels to the whole world. They constitute the new Bible in the age of Spirit. When this teaching is incorporated into our daily lives, we begin to experience our first nature. Our second nature belongs to the flesh, whose time has come to an end and is passed away forever. We now come into the new life and the new condition promised to us by our LORD Jesus Christ. He is the one who built a bridge from mortality to immortality. He said on the cross, "It is finished." For that reason, the former things have passed away, even though it took two thousand years to fulfill them. In the age of Spirit, there is only eternity. For that reason, two thousand years is like a moment in time. Don't forget we are immersed in the dispensation of time.

Now we move from the foot of the cross to the open tomb. Where can this baptism of fire be obtained? Alas, not in your local church or denomination. For this baptism is not found there. This baptism can be given by anyone who received the same. If you have been baptized before, you received the baptism of John the Baptist for repentance and it is valued. Are we not all sinners? Do we not all need repentance for ours sins? But as we now move into the time of Spirit, we embrace the baptism of fire for the forgiveness of all our sins. In this generation, the Holy Spirit is coming for the righteous. After the remission of sins, you are righteous before God, your Father. I can tell you quite inevitably, if your own spirit desires this baptism, you have to ask for it. Believe it is yours. Our loving Father will open the way for you. For this God searches our heart and mind and knows all things. He knows His children and calls them by name. Ask and you shall receive. As a spiritual mother, I want all of you to have the understanding that you must ask properly. It is not enough just to ask. You must ask in the name that is operative in the age of Spirit. In the past, it was wonderful to ask in the name of our LORD Jesus Christ, but even that name so powerful comes under the umbrella of the new name of God. This new name is a universal name that applies to every tribe and tongue, to every spiritual discipline, to all created things. Use it in this age of Spirit, and you will be amazed about the results that will manifest in your life. Be wise, and understand what our LORD Jesus Christ meant when He said, "You do not receive, because you do not ask aright (properly)." I do not wish any of our Father's children to miss the incredible blessings of the spiritual age of the Son of Man. Use this new name Olumba O. Obu and test it yourself. Nothing succeeds like success. My love surrounds each and every one of you, in the name of the Holy Trinity. Amen.

Sister Beverly Marts

Introduction

A new era has started. A marvelous light is taking away bondage that made us suffer.

Light makes darkness disappear; nothing can hide from it. Evil deeds are being uncovered; secrets are being revealed. Nothing and no one is irrelevant to God. He is no respecter of persons. The universal message will always be directed to the need that exists in each person's heart and mind. This message will ring a bell. It will make the transition from the impersonal to the personal.

Our own spirit will bear witness. Let us take what is ours, and leave the rest. This universal message invariably finds its mark and is intended to carry out our true assignment. The Holy Spirit is interacting with us in a new way. He is walking with us and talking to us all the time.

Every corner of the world is impacted by His divine authority, whether we realize it or not, whether we know Him or not.

This book is for all mankind; it has special relevance for the reconnection of the universal sisterhood and the equality of man. God asks His children all over the world to come closer to His heart. We are a lucky generation.

Thank you, Father.

Universal Sisterhood

A woman opens her mouth with wisdom and on her tongue is the law of kindness.

Proverbs 31:26

"Men have always ruled the world, but this is all over now, because we girls are coming, and believe me, we are coming in a storm."

Those were the words of a South African teenage girl at the groundbreaking ceremonies of the Oprah Winfrey Leadership Academy for Girls in Johannesburg, South Africa. Oprah said, "This is a supreme moment of destiny." Through this act of kindness, leaders will arise from that small beginning and will spread like wildfire throughout the world.

This young girl spoke not of her own, but gave the world a great revelation from God for the coming time.

A New Beginning

The new millennium sings to women and all of humanity a song of new beginnings. Nature renews herself continually; humans are also constantly changing and growing. In this new era, most of us search for a greater meaning in life, believing the universe has something great for each and every one of us. The impact of the tragedy on September 11, 2001, left an uneasy feeling in us. That manmade disaster changed many of us. Any tragic event will jolt us out of our complacency.

A broader picture is emerging that is awakening us to a more spiritual life. September 11 was a thunderbolt because we had been on automatic pilot for a long time. Many of us promised to change, to look at life differently. We are now challenged to rise from our individual concerns to a broader picture of humanity. We can see that we are not alone in this world, but have brothers and sisters who are suffering greatly. We are compelled to help them, to make their lives easier. Our heavenly Father does not like to see His people suffer. He likes to see joy on all our faces.

Our LORD Jesus Christ came to make this world a better place and taught us to love one another. Through this new insight, we understand that we must learn to get along. Let us see this new beginning as a glorious opportunity to go forward in the love of God. This *love* was always with us, but we did not recognize it all the time, or in many cases, we rejected it. Love will start a new awareness in us. This newly found love must be applied in our daily lives. This will transform the human experience greatly and will bring us to a higher level of awareness. We are walking away from the old to a more fulfilling life. One cannot bring the old thinking into the new era. We will use our valuable time for great causes.

We, as a people, will become more gentle and appreciative toward one another. Any tragedy, may it be on a national or personal level, brings us to new understandings. In this new millennium, we will enter a new greatness as a people. Some might say they have not seen any changes. Yet every journey starts with a first step. Great inventions are coming our way and will be everyday events. Unknown mysteries start to unravel. During the evolution of man, great teachers appeared at different times and in different countries. In our time, many will come to new understandings all at once. This is the greatest time to be on this planet. Our souls have waited for this time.

What Does The Universal Sisterhood Represent?

The word *universal* means "we sing a song in unison." This song is all-encompassing and has many verses. A universal sisterhood comes in love, never with force. We represent the new life and the new condition. This is the time of liberation for all creation, a cosmic turning point in the scheme of things. We sisters know that the power we are coming with is from above and that no man can shut the door. We will succeed this time with strength unknown to any movement. This song that will be sung all over the world will move us from a theoretical to a hands-on application.

As the gates open wide, women are standing at the entrance, contemplating what to do next. We are demanding nothing less than total liberation for women all over the world. There is a time for everything under the sun, and our time is now. Universally united we stand strong. The power of this movement is begging description for it is indescribable. Women have moved from a position of weakness to a position of strength. Once men understand that they are only playing with half a deck of cards, will they not request all the missing cards to be put into play? They'll guide their steps to gladly include the other half to be complete. Women will break the chain of abuse once they learn and put into practice the power that is theirs by divine right. We can only be fully liberated with God's blessings. We are His daughters, and we have been with Him from the beginning. Our true position is neither negotiable nor questionable; it is what it is. This spiritual liberation gives us the authority to move forward. We are one!

Women Are At the Forefront

As changes occur on earth, women are at the forefront. Our nurturing spirits are necessary for lasting change. Growth in anything comes from following a plan. Women have a natural ability to handle relationships with all, including the opposite gender. We are surrounded by a special aura of love. We are coming from years of hardships and are marching toward our victory. The drama of moving forward had its own consequences in the past, but now the doors are wide open, and we are not looking back. Women in the western world have had their physical liberation, but now the time has come for the spiritual liberation. One is not complete without the other. Our goal is total liberation. We are not totally free until every woman on earth is liberated. If only some of us are liberated, we have not reached our goal. The world listens to women with high profiles. It is their assignment to step forward and take part in this mighty work. Far-reaching impacts will follow. Truly, in the eyes of God, we were never victims but always His beloved children, engaged in making a better life not only for our own children, but also for the entire world.

> Many women have done excellently, but you surpass them all.
>
> Proverbs 31:29

This Generation Will Surpass Them All

Yes, we surpass them all by looking forward and by forgiving our oppressors. Let us now look to tomorrow and see what plan our heavenly Father has for His daughters. Our trials before this long-awaited freedom have been completed. The karma has been paid. There is a beginning for everything under the sun and there is also an ending. We have not become complacent or unchallenged. We paid our dues. Women through the centuries grew weary from the pain, and it forced them to cast their eyes down. The few who raised their eyes to seek a new path led the way for our independence, allowing the women of today to look life squarely in the eye. Now the door has opened beyond the pain, which ignited our courage and has given us understanding for others and compassion for our fellow human beings. This means a new life and a new condition. Women in the western world have long thought they were free and liberated, but their spiritual understanding is only now beginning.

Find the spirit of love in your heart.

Women Are Victorious

> And there appeared a great wonder in heaven, a woman clothed with the sun, and the moon under her feet, and upon her head a crown of twelve stars.
>
> Revelation 12:1

The woman in Revelation 12:1 shows us that the journey of Eve was a successful one. She is victorious at the end, for a crown was handed to her. She is the queen of heaven, but also of earth. The sun and moon under her feet show us that she overcame the earthly things. The twelve stars represent the twelve tribes of Israel. Our first mother, Eve, led all women throughout time to total victory.

This journey has made us strong for this time, which was destined from time immemorial. Adversity changes people; it gives them a new insight. Once perceptions change, new possibilities present themselves. One emerges stronger from travail and limitations. Are you not a new person? Most women understand themselves; they have the talent for introspection and know where they come from and where they are going. Through this divine understanding, the drama of the "second-class citizen" has ended. The new time has begun.

We have been confused about our roles as women and about taking our rightful places. Women are more than willing to help planet earth in this new stage of evolution. It has never been about a man opening our doors, nor was it about how much we can lift. Because of this confusion, some took advantage of women. Women themselves were unsure of their positions. Certain women played roles that men had designed for them. In this generation, women walk away from those roles to follow their own intuitions. They try to create their own role in society. No matter what women try in the future, no matter what office they choose to attain, they will succeed. Let us support one another in every endeavor. Once we unite, we are a powerful and immovable force.

Coming from a family of seven girls, I like to be around women. Also I am a woman that went through many years of domestic violence, which brought me to the place where I am today. It gave me the opportunity of becoming a person of great insight. If one has not gone through fire, one does not know how hot the flames can be. My wings had been clipped, but just like many of you, they have grown stronger and allow me to soar.

However, all this is not the reason for this book. I had a divine calling to be a student of a great spiritual teacher, Olumba O. Obu, from the nation of Nigeria. He is telling the whole world it is now time to love one another. Through him, I learned to first forgive myself and then forgive those who wronged me and love all creation. His divine wisdom is far above earthly wisdom. He is the one who decreed that the time for liberation of women is now.

Our Time Is Here

Women of the world, without a doubt, our time is here. Those who are still in slavery, hold on, your time for liberation has come. The reality is that *love* will rule. We will not bargain away our new position or be evasive about it. We have come to recognize ourselves. We are here to stay. We will be at the forefront of life-changing events in the world. Our input will be of utmost importance. The world cannot go forward without half the population. This is a great victory and has moved us from heartbreak to total triumph.

The spiritual liberation is the true "aha moment" for women. Truly, our fundamental goal was predestined from the beginning of time. The journey that women went through is an astonishing one. My spiritual mother said that this journey gives us strength for this time. This maturity comes only from hardship. Once we understand our circumstances, the tragedy ends. The only victims here are those who stand in our way. Repression invites karma, which brings pain and regret to the oppressor. We shall move from law to grace.

As Sister Beverly states, "Our mundane world is the plane of effect. The spirit world is the plane of cause." We will rule our environment with peace, love, joy, and harmony, which emanate from the Spirit. Once we know our authentic self, we are empowered. Our super conscious mind, the mind of Christ within, will lead us. It has neither a beginning nor an end. Once we find that this truth is found richly in our hearts, it will be evident in our daily lives. This is the age of the Spirit. Our souls will be at the forefront and clamor for quality time. Ignoring the soul would have catastrophic consequences.

Laugh women, for our time has come! We have been set free many years ago on the physical level; the spiritual freedom must follow and is here. As the spiritual mother is set free, so are her daughters all over the world set free. Those are defining moments in the new millennium, moments that are life changing. The fence is now behind us. This forces us to take a new look at ourselves to see who we are and to check out where we are going. The pain of yesteryear will disappear as we grow stronger. The piercing intensity of disillusionment from the past left us doubting ourselves.

We are experiencing this defining moment individually as well as collectively, and its impact is being felt all over the world. Let us unite in this circle of sisterhood, and let us share our feelings and thoughts. It is exciting to see where this new role will lead us. The road will be cleared for us as we dare to move forward with this new God-given freedom. Nobody will ever dim our light again. Yes, we have broken the bondage which once had suppressed us. We are accepting this new role with a thankful heart. Once this freedom has found a place in our hearts, it will not disappear any more. The previous darkness will be forgotten as though it never existed.

I Had a Dream In 2003

I saw thousands of women in a huge lobby waiting for an escalator to take them to a higher level in a big building. They were anxious to make this journey. A few people, including my spiritual mother and myself, were waiting on the higher level for them to join us. As I looked down, all I could see was a big field of flowers in every color of the rainbow. Their clothing showed me that all were women.

This dream was given to me in Florida, the land of light. This was a revelation of things to come, and it means that women are anxious to move to a higher level of spirituality.

> Commit thy works unto the LORD, and thy thoughts shall be established.
>
> Proverbs 16:3

The Light Is Shining On Women

When our Father opens doors, no one can close them. God opens the doors for His daughters and allows the light to shine upon them. Therefore, we can step boldly onto this new ground. We have the spiritual duty to help our sisters in other countries to alleviate oppression of old traditions and cultures, so that they, too, can reach freedom and step into the light. What great joy it is for us to help our sisters in this struggle for the betterment of planet earth. It is a holy duty, a royal assignment.

The pain we women endure to bring forth new life and perpetuate love and kindness shows true humanity. We are merely expressing our true selves for the betterment of this planet. The changes have to start in our own hearts and minds.

Women, know this is your time; stop your weeping, and hold your heads up high. Is it not amazing that we let men rule over us—the very men we brought into this world?

Let love open the door.

Women Bring Forth Life

> Strength and honor are her clothing and she shall rejoice in the time to come.
>
> Proverbs 31:25

> *As the channel of life women should be respected. Even God chose this channel to come to earth.*

Women were given the mission to bring forth life. The creation process of new life allows another spirit to return to earth to start its earthly journey. It is a woman who will give of herself; her tongue teaches the law of kindness and love. A spirit that moves into the womb of a woman is surrounded by water at all times because the child's spirit is fire. The energy of birth naturally prompts a mother's nurturing, and brings forth a new life. New lives begin continually in this world. This assignment from our Father is a gift of great importance to all women and humanity. A woman's love, persistence, education, and communication open doors for a child. Pain is endured with patience as the pregnancy brings the hope for another life.

Most women are programmed by nature to bear children, and with a song in their hearts, they bring forth life. Even though providing children with a bridge from the spiritual into the physical world is fraught with pain, this is the ultimate gift to the world. A miracle develops in the womb as loving beings merge in the dance of life.

> *God chose women to give the precious gift of life.*
> *They are His caretakers of peace and joy.*

A Universal Sister

Phoebe White, a universal sister, mother, artist, healer, and counselor wrote these words:

> Women are fantastically magical creatures made primarily of love. They are designed to manifest life itself. They are also equipped with a magnificent spectrum of emotional depth and compassion. Women offer a kaleidoscope of natural gifts innate within their biological physiology and spiritual fabric. They are beings of great aptitude, endearment, inspiration, and influence.

Women have been assigned by Mother Nature to show that love is the most sought-after, valuable, and powerful force in the world. A woman's inherent nature is to love, nurture, protect, inspire, empathize, mold, nourish, comfort, and influence. As a mother to future generations, she embodies devotion, commitment, sacrifice, positive influence, companionship, prudence, and love. She nourishes the mind, body, and spirit of her children.

Throughout history, women have been highly regarded as the positive influences and constant support of many famous and successful men, including presidents and great rulers around the world.

Women have accomplished great feats throughout history as they played their many roles as inventors, scientists, politicians, designers, pilots, actresses, philanthropists, and saints. Women today, in every job and walk of life, are recognizing their true identities.

> *In celebration of our heart and soul, we have recognized that the love of a women is a constant force in our life.*

Who Are We?

It is of great importance to help each other realize who we are and where we are going. We will have insight into how much work is needed for us to grow. First, we must realize that we are connected to the time, place, culture, and customs of our heritage. Conditioning starts early as our truths come from different sources. We all are innocent at birth. As children of the universe, it is our birthright to be nurtured and loved. However, this is not always the case.

Since the beginning, our souls have been longing for harmony, cooperation, sharing, and reverence of life. When our consciousness changes to the awareness of the great powers we hold within, we will reconnect to our source energy, which is this loving universe. Our hearts' desires will be met again. We will be truly one when there is no more division between man and woman. In time, we will realize that to be on this planet is all about the growth of our souls. We are spiritual beings having human experiences. As adults, we are filled with fears and doubts, but once we become trusting and loving like children again, we become new creatures in Christ.

> I have said, ye are gods; and all of you are children of the most high.
>
> Psalms 82:6

We Will Become the Race of Light

The era is closing during which we received or acquired our power from material things that defined us by our looks and/or by how far we could reach for the materialistic life. Every day, people worried about their daily bread, how to survive, and how to keep up with the Joneses. In the future, we will balance our lives; we will worry about our souls. We will let go of our past mistakes and the habits we acquired, for we are all here for the same reasons. We will not hang our heads in desperation anymore. We will raise our heads and look toward the stars. See how they move in their orderly way; they do not jump and leave their tracks. Let us breathe deeply, and let us consider that we are here for a great reason. God knew the prophet Jeremiah in his mother's womb. He also knows us from our mother's womb. Let us not miss this opportunity to discover unknown powers within ourselves, which we always had. Let us reach for them now.

We will move from fear, distrust, and confusion to love, peace, and inner joy. Wake up, humanity! The sky is not the ceiling; the sky is only the beginning. We are experiencing a new time and a new condition on this planet. A powerful presence is directing the whole operation. As we are contemplating what to do, a new wind is already blowing upon this planet. No one can oppose the supernatural force.

We are like birds that learn to fly. Taking that first step comes naturally. Babies do it all the time; they never fail. We have imposed our own limitations. Those who went before us showed us the way. We are not growing apart. We are coming together.

Some of us are afraid to express our voices in fear of being ridiculed or rejected in society, yet there are others who speak up with a strong voice. We have been conditioned to conform to our environment, home, school, and church. To be different is frowned upon, which suppresses contact with our real self. To repress feelings, to ignore and deny them, is not in our best interest. Substance abuse of any kind, whether it is alcohol, drugs, or medications, serves to hide our own true selves. Our bodies as well as our emotions are composed of energy. We perceive outside stimuli with our emotional body first. We play the game of life, which is largely make-believe. We get caught up in our own vain ideals and images. When pain enters our body, we receive a wake-up call. When we repress our real feelings, we create an opportunity for sickness to take over. We must learn to understand ourselves.

We have forgotten that we are energy in motion. When we store emotional pain, we create blockages of energy. Doubt and fear become trapped in our cells. Once we let go of these emotions, our life force flows abundantly again. Let us be aware of these interactions and act accordingly. This knowledge can bring a great transformation in itself. Let go of the emotional pain, and reconnect to the universal energy. We must get in touch with our inner, wounded, emotional body. We must learn to forgive ourselves and forgive those whose actions have caused us pain. The negative patterns must end.

Forgiveness brings peace and the healing necessary for us to be the whole person we were created to be. As we are filled with love, we become the most powerful healing tool—not only for ourselves, but for the world.

One out of every four women is battered in this country. How is this possible in a First World nation?

Women, as well as men, will come out of this condition. To allow any abuse will be incomprehensible in the future. By allowing another human being to take our power away, we are giving permission to this person to take it. We are coming out of bondage and are being released from old patterns of negativity. That we have accepted this pattern as inevitable is a sad commentary on our behavior and society.

To Love One Another is a law in this age. (or: the new age.)

Imagine Your Future

When we imagine something, it is within our mind. Energy is being moved, and action is created. We can therefore change our reality by focusing our minds. The earth is in constant change caused by wind, fire, and shifting lands, which keep it in constant movement. This change is also within us. We are always evolving to a higher plane of existence. If we are not aware of this change, we live unconsciously. Once we open our minds to positive thoughts, we will accept all of God's creation and reconnect to one another. We are all universal children who are loved and treasured from above. It is not by accident that the book, *The Secret*, was rediscovered in our time. That universal secret has always been there for God's children.

We must realize that through love, companionship, and commitment, we can make a major difference for everyone we come in contact with and, hence, the whole planet. Let us all grow in positive strength, love, and wisdom so that we may lift up our world into a place of peace and joy for all.

As women have we stepped up to the challenge? We have great jobs and own our houses, but still feel incomplete without a man.

We do not need to be with just any man to make us feel complete. We are already complete. Should the right man come our way for that divine union, then we are ready to be with a man. Every woman knows in her heart who her perfect partner is. Some of us have sought men in all the wrong places. Sometimes it is in our life plan to have children, other times it is not. The true design comes from our higher self and was decided before we were born. Take heart! The good news is that our bondage has been removed. All is well.

Following is part of an address given to the Universal Women's Fellowship meeting by Olumba O. Obu, the chairman of the Brotherhood of the Cross and Star in Calabar, Nigeria:

> Women Are Called To Be Peacemakers
>
> Let the profound peace and grace of our Father be with you in the name of our Lord Jesus Christ, Amen.
>
> I welcome all to the Universal Women's Fellowship meeting. It gives me great joy to be in your midst to deliver further information about our collective interest, which anchors solely on building the kingdom of God. The role of the woman from creation on has been

that of tending, nurturing, and managing any condition, situation, and circumstance tactfully with the singular aim of gradually developing and establishing an acceptable and preferable standard. Women have always existed as useful vessels for development and innovative advances; hence, a home without a woman can hardly be sustained.

In recognition of this quality possessed by women, they have been called out of the world to perform a singular role in the kingdom of God. To succeed in this role, women must possess and exhibit love. Women the world over are coming together in unity and understanding. These qualities are ever indicative of success and bring achievements. Therefore, it is wise to implore the multitude of women to be appreciative to the Father for His love, care, guidance, good health, and protection. The victory over all principalities of darkness is granted to His daughters in the name of our LORD Jesus Christ. Amen.

Lack of love and unity has oftentimes hampered women's envisioned goals; hence, they are encouraged to embrace unity and show unconditional love towards one another. You have been called as co-laborers by the Father to build the kingdom of God and propel it higher. Therefore, show exceeding joy and gladness for this honor that is bestowed upon you.

In the course of the advice and blessings to all women, I have expressed regret over the lack of knowledge in regard to women's identities. The failure to realize who they are and the responsibilities that they have been charged with has greatly deterred them from performing their duties. Therefore, the blessings could not follow them. The Father has demonstrated much love and sympathy for women. This magnitude of love suggests that women should rise up with great vigor and show their appreciation for all He has done for them.

The Father mandates women to institute peace on earth. Progress reports will come out of this. It makes one wonder what is holding women back from playing their divine roles.

There is no lengthy speech needed, because the basic role is laid out for women. The building of the kingdom of God and instituting peace on earth is clearly spelled out by the Father. What is now expected is results that are brought on through the love women will exhibit. The kingdom of God is a moving train. Move along with it, or you will be left behind.

Let all the women bear in mind that through their work in the kingdom of God, their salvation and glory is worked out. All women have been set free of their ailments, court cases, and problems of the world. They are blessed according to their works.

Let the Father's peace and blessings abide with the whole world, now and forevermore. Amen.

Traditions in Other Countries

> Thy hands have made me and fashioned me: give me understanding, that I may learn thy commandments.
>
> Psalms 119:73

Hunger, disease, and sickness prevail due to lack of funds and knowledge in many countries; so some men, women, and children who are living in these conditions become victims of sexual bondage and slavery. They suffer because not enough is done to bring relief to their plight. We learn of their sufferings from news and television reports by people who actively seek to expose the cases where physical and emotional freedoms are denied. Unfortunately, even in the West, sexual slavery is taking place. In some countries, men dominate women who do not have the physical freedom that we enjoy in the western world. These women are still subjugated to their husbands in all things, including their clothing.

In certain countries, the tradition of mutilating young girls is still practiced. Women of the world, how can we sit quietly and do nothing? God created women. How can we allow a tradition to harm and terminate a woman's right to physical and mental health? This brutality is forced on innocent children by traditions that control and inherently destroy the respect between men and women and leave women disfigured and in pain for life. Let us help stop this by any means possible.

There are customs in which women become outcasts of their own families when they try to escape from emotionally and physically abusive husbands. Some girls are forced to marry and bear children while they are still children themselves. Their own families, who do not want them to become a burden, sell them. Others are given to a man's family with a large dowry, and if he chooses not to want her, he can send her back and keep the dowry. Women are killed or maimed by their in-laws so they will not be able to find another husband. The welfare of their children in these circumstances is not considered.

In some countries, women may be killed by their own families for dishonoring their husbands. Women are stoned to death when they are accused of fornication. Yet this punishment is not meted out to men who commit the same offence.

All women will have physical, as well as spiritual, freedom when the women of the world band together to finally stop these old traditions. God, our Father, will be on our side to accomplish this task. Once the perpetrators have reached a higher consciousness, they will stay away from old traditions.

A bumper sticker says, "Women are born leaders, you are following one."

Women Have a Nurturing Spirit

In the age of Spirit, we do not only sympathize with those less fortunate in the world, but we also help them. Women have natural gifts from God like nurturing, comforting, and care-taking to alleviate pain and suffering. How can we appreciate what others go through unless we had the same experience?

Oprah Winfrey stated in an interview with Diane Sawyer about her work in Africa that she feels she would be judged if she did not help. She chose to provide school supplies for children, money for teachers who had given of their own time to teach the children, and funds to build schools.

There are many different ways of helping. We all can help in a big or a small way. The opportunity to help the less fortunate is leading to great triumphs of the soul. Our soul reveals to us our higher purpose. We all go through an inescapable school of learning on planet earth that gives us our depth. There is a purpose for each and every one of us. Let us not throw away our time on how we look or how much we weigh, but let us use it in every way for the betterment of the world. Not to help the less fortunate would put us under judgment.

On a Tyra Banks's show, Tyra noted that women are breaking bonds instead of strengthening them. She called this the "seven sins women commit towards each other"—betrayal, manipulation, judging, envy, gossip, competition, and resentment. All these things are not from our Father; they are from the other side, which is called the "negative side." Who, then, are we serving if we behave this way? Where is the spirit of sisterhood?

On one of Oprah's shows while discussing women's relationships, it was said that women have "holes in their hearts." Truly, whole generations of women cry out to be healed. We are so often treated as objects. Women are losing the opportunity to show the world what they can do and what they can accomplish. Men are bored with women who can bring nothing to a relationship. Where are the role models for our young people? Television commercials show what young women have to do to please a man. Women of the world, what is going on?

> Let every soul be subject unto the higher powers. For there is no power but of God: the powers that be are of God.
>
> Romans 13:1

Girlfriends Make the World a Better Place

An uplifting article, "Girlfriends Make the World a Better Place," by Debby Wood has been written in the newspaper called *The Shopper*. This article mentioned,

> Don't forget your girlfriends. They'll be more important as you get older. No matter how much you love your husband, no matter how much you love the children you'll have, you are still going to need girlfriends. Remember to go places with them. And remember that girlfriends are not only your friends, but your sisters, your daughters, and other relatives, too. You need other women. Women always do.
>
> As time and nature work their changes and their mysteries upon a woman, girlfriends are the mainstay of her life. After fifty years, I learned that time passes, life happens, and distance separates. Children grow up, love waxes and wanes, and hearts break. Careers end, jobs come and go, parents die, colleagues forget favors, and men don't call when they say they will. But girlfriends are there, no matter how much time and how many miles are between them. A girlfriend is never farther away than the need to reach her.
>
> When we have to walk that lonesome valley and we have to walk it by ourselves, our girlfriends will be at the valley's rim, cheering us on, praying for us, pulling for us, intervening on our behalf, and waiting with open arms

at the valley's end. Sometimes they will even break the rules and walk beside us or come in and carry us out.

Daughters, sisters, mothers, sisters-in-law, mothers-in-law, aunts, nieces, cousins, extended family, co-workers, and friends bless our life. The world would not be the same without them. When we began this adventure called womanhood, we had no idea of the incredible joys or sorrows that lay ahead. Nor did we know how much we need each other. Every day, we need each other still. Let the women in our life know how much they are appreciated. Start each day with a laugh.

Behind Every Successful Woman Is Herself

Friendships among Women

At UCLA, a study was conducted on friendship among women. It was noted that friendships among women are very special. They shape who we are and who we are yet to be. They soothe our tumultuous inner world, fill the emotional gap in our marriage, and help us remember who we really are. Scientists now suspect that hanging out with our friends can actually counteract the stress that most of us experience on a daily basis.

The discovery that women respond to stress differently than men was made in a classic "aha moment" shared by two female scientists who were talking one day in a lab at UCLA. They shared this joke that when women who worked in the lab were stressed, they came in, cleaned the lab, had coffee, and bonded. When men were stressed, they holed up somewhere on their own.

A health study from Harvard Medical School found that the more friends women had, the less likely they were to develop physical impairments as they aged and the more likely they were to lead a joyful life. In fact, the results were so significant that the researchers concluded that not having close friends and confidants was as detrimental to their health as smoking or carrying extra weight.

Women can be formidable supporters of each other. They nurture each other. Women need space and time in which to have talks with other women, which can be healing experiences.

I have never heard a man ask for advice on how to combine marriage and a career.

> And the servant of the beneficent God are they who walk on earth in humbleness, and when the ignorant address them, say: peace.
>
> The Koran 25:63

Forgiveness

> For his eyes are upon the ways of man, and he seeth all his goings.
>
> Job 34:21

When events in the world disrupt our lives, we can allow this to redirect our purpose or teach us to understand the human condition. This is the time when we reach out to our loved ones and friends for comfort, but we also need to extend that comfort to others. This moves humanity to a more fulfilling role. The changes that are all around us are representative of our collective consciousness. Nothing happens without purpose. There are no accidents or coincidences in the spiritual or the physical world.

Women and all humans are divine children of an eternal Father. When something happens on earth, it is brought about by the collective frame of mind at that time and in that space. There are many lessons to be learned. Women the world over have done so much to advance the work on earth that one can only marvel that our spirits have not been dimmed. In the present time, women are expected to hold a job and care for children. Many raise children by themselves and keep their households running with their myriad chores like cooking, shopping, cleaning, washing, driving, etc. No wonder we are worn out mentally, physically, and spiritually, which leaves little time for the soul.

We Have a Divine Heritage

In the age of Spirit, we are given time to rediscover our divine heritage—the purpose of our journey on earth. Our lovely soul waited for us so patiently. We will learn that one cannot do everything. Some know this truth, live by it, and are able to say no.

As we view the immensity of events around the world, we become aware of coming changes. Humans generally do not like change. We do not like to bend when a mighty wind blows, but we must, for this change is necessary. The events are like pieces of a puzzle, but soon we will see a beautiful picture emerging.

Every philosophical teaching tells us that love and peace start within us. When will love find a way into our hearts? We must search for love within ourselves, where we also find peace, joy, patience, tolerance, compassion, empathy, and all great virtues of the spirit. We know that the greatest is *love*.

> A woman stretcheth out her hand to the poor,
> and reaches forth her hand to the needy.
>
> Proverbs 31:20

Let Us Forgive All

As women all over the world get together to celebrate their new freedom, let us first go on our knees and ask for the forgiveness of our sins. Then let us forgive those who wronged us. Only then can our healing begin. The gentle man from Galilee showed us how to forgive two thousand years ago. There is no other way to heal our wounds. Even if something seemingly unforgivable was done to us, let us forgive the perpetrator and ourselves. We need to forgive because we all need forgiveness. Forgiveness stops the suffering, hurt, and remembrance of the deeds. Let us forgive in order to heal and work through the pain and, as a result, put it behind us. Forgiveness is for the healing of ourselves: our bodies, minds, and souls. Let us not rehash the same incidents over and over in our minds. We have control over our minds. The mind does not control us. Forgiveness sets us free.

Let us forgive ourselves out of compassion for ourselves. Forgiveness is an act of self-love. Some divorced women become physically sick when they hear the name of their ex-husbands. Let us forgive the injustices that were done to us. The perpetrators might not have known how to do better. Most men think and feel differently than women, as described in the book by Dr. John Gray, *Men are from Mars, Women are from Venus*.

We have forgiven ourselves when there is no more emotional reaction at the mentioning of the perpetrator's name or when we touch the wound and it does not hurt anymore. There will always be scars, and we will have the memory of what happened, but it won't hurt any longer.

Some might say, "It's easy to say one should forgive, but I have tried, and I cannot do it." They have determined in their minds that this particular case cannot be forgiven. The truth is, they want to hold on to their pain and therefore do not want to forgive. However, forgiveness is first and foremost for one's own benefit. Pray to the heavenly Father for the ability to forgive others.

As little children playing with our friends, forgiveness was instinctive. We always forgave, time after time. Do we remember how effortlessly we forgave? Right away in most instances. We do not need to learn to forgive because we were born with the capacity to forgive. We have learned how not to forgive and seem to do it so well. Now if we don't like what is done to us, we say, "Forget it. They are out of my life." We like to add, "Who needs this?" This used to be my saying, as well, which is a sign of pride. We think that a certain trespass is unforgivable, but we are the ones who suffer and add salt to our own wounds. We elevate suffering to an art form.

If it is the other way around and someone forgives us for our wrongdoing, we are very sorrowful and may even shed some tears. We should go back to our childhood and reconnect with the little girl or boy we were, who could so easily forgive. Let us make a list of everybody we need to ask for forgiveness. Then we kneel and ask our heavenly Father to help us to forgive. Remember, the actions done against us are merely the demons in the other person's mind. Let us not take it personally. Once we have that awareness, we will find compassion and understanding in our hearts. Let us practice forgiveness, which then will become easier and easier. Once we forgive, self-acceptance and self-love can, and does, begin. The supreme forgiveness is to forgive oneself. We don't need to suffer anymore or pay anymore. It can be over.

Our LORD Jesus Christ said, "If you cannot forgive others, I cannot forgive you." What a statement! It has touched my heart. It is of utmost importance that God forgives me. After I became aware of the necessity to forgive, forgiveness became easier. Do not think that the person we forgave will get away with anything. "Vengeance is Mine, I will repay," says the LORD (Deuteronomy 32:35). He will deal with wrongdoers so much better because they are also His children who need to learn lessons in life. God saves every tear we cry. Once we have forgiven, we speed up the healing process through love. There is no other medicine that heals better than unconditional love.

Women all over the world, let us all forgive the men and women who have hurt us because we want to move forward. Also, we want to be clean before our God. Let the women of the world celebrate a national forgiveness day. Let us ask the Spirit to choose the right time and the right person for this assignment. It would be such a life-changing occurrence for women. Of course, men are always welcome to join.

> Our Heavenly Father is Asking His Daughters to Come Closer to His Heart.

We Have an Eternal Father

Life is never-ending, for we are all energy, which is like electricity. Just because one electrical outlet is destroyed does not mean energy stops. In fact, it still flows freely. Energy can be changed but never destroyed, whether in this nor in the next world.

In this day and time, anything is possible. When heaven and earth merge together, we become celestial beings. There will be no more limits. We always had wings. We are spirits who had to come here to learn and complete an assignment, which may be great or small. When our assignment is carried out in love, we triumph over our own mortality and progress toward our destiny.

We are challenged, we are confronted, and we are frustrated, but it is in suffering that we become strong and learn our lessons well. Through our challenges, the mystery that is called "life" is revealed to us. In the process, we hopefully play the game of life well.

We are one divine family, and we are world citizens. Our differences should be celebrated continually. We have let others do the thinking for us and have accepted mass consciousness. Now the light is shining upon us; the spirit of love is poured over us and seeks to reestablish peace and unity.

The complacency and old patterns are broken. We now realize that we must change. Out of this human learning, we are given the opportunity to reach for heights we have never known before. We are going back to our Father's heart. He is leading us to a new heaven and a new earth where righteousness dwells. He is waiting for us.

> Show me thy ways, O Lord; teach me thy paths.
> Psalms 25:4

Humankind's Rightful Position

> Be strong and bold; have no fear or dread of them, because it is the LORD your God who goes with you; he will not fail you or forsake you.
>
> Deuteronomy 31:6

Women Are Helping To Make the World A Better Place

When Hillary Clinton was a senator, she was a guest of honor at a graduation for an Atlanta area women's college. Senator Clinton told graduates of the liberal arts institution that all women must make a contribution to the world, saying,

> You cannot have freedom if half the people are told at birth they are inferior. You cannot

> have peace when half the people authoritatively decide how the other half should live. So it is imperative that we not just rhetorically stand for peace and freedom and democracy, but that we work to help educate young women to take their places in free democratic societies that will be friends and allies of the United States for years to come.

Hillary Clinton helps educate young women all over the world so that peace, freedom, and democracy can reign. It is imperative that we help. To be regarded as inferior because one is female needs to become a thing of the past. Hillary Clinton will be at the forefront of movements that help humanity, whichever position she holds.

We pray for men and women everywhere who are serving humanity by putting their personal dreams aside and bringing comfort to others. I pray for them, for their assignment was given to them before they were born. They are following God's will and listening to His voice. We need to pray for all world leaders. Did God not give them their jobs? If they fail their assignments, we all will suffer. Their choices affect not only their lives, but also the lives of all people around the world. World leaders need to be open to God's guidance. If they fail to accomplish their assignments or put their own welfare first, then people will suffer, and they will have to answer to God.

Former First Lady Hillary Clinton wanted to bring healthcare to all Americans, which is a subject close to her heart. However, she was overruled at the time. So many people in this country are without healthcare. During low points in their lives, when they cannot help themselves or their families, their government should be there for them. This is a great tragedy, which is allowed in a First World country. People are at their wits' end. Many are left to suffer, and it is tearing families apart. It has caused many to lose everything they worked for during their lives. During times of worry about health, they have to agonize about bill collectors and/or selling the house. They are told to talk to the hospital about paying their bills according to their means. Are we only getting sick once? In many cases, once a sickness starts, complications follow. This great injustice will have consequences for the responsible parties. The women of today will change this great wrong. They will fight for help for their families during times of sickness. Strives are being made for a better future of the healthcare system.

Childcare is another example of the defenselessness of single mothers and families. There is no plan or help for working mothers. Americans are told that this is the greatest country to live in, yet they don't know what benefits people in other countries receive from their governments. Let Americans be educated about this, and let their government match the childcare that is enjoyed in other countries.

> Deceit is in the heart of them that imagine evil:
> but to the counselors of peace is joy.
>
> Proverbs 12:20

Crimes against each other have to stop in the time of the Spirit; otherwise, societies will not move forward because they have not learned anything.

To love one another is the law in this new millennium. In one of my books, called *Love, the Spiritual Journey*, I mention, "As we are yet standing in silence, contemplating what to do next, love has entered our hearts." We are returning to love; it will ignite in our hearts.

We Walk Away From Bondage

From now on, men and women will walk away from bondage, which we entered into in the garden of Eden. The time of sorrow and the time for men to rule physically over women has passed. We are moving into the time of Spirit. We have been so busy chasing our worldly goals that we neglected our eternal souls. With this door opening, it is time for us to just be.

> I will greatly multiply thy sorrow and thy conception; in sorrow thou shall bring forth children; and thy desire shall be to thy husband, and he shall rule over thee.
>
> Genesis 3:16

A Man's Rightful Position

Is not a man held in bondage also when he subjugates his mate? Of course he is. Liberation is his, too, lest he be lost in this human tragedy as well. Behaving like an oppressor puts him in a perceived position of strength, but in reality, it shows his weakness. How can there be victory for him when he brings pain and creates division? God, our Father, has not forgotten anyone. He restores men to their rightful place. Men will again accept the role of partner, protector, provider and nurturer and be an active participant in his family and community. This is a male's rightful place.

All Things Hidden Must Come Into the Light

The liberation of women around the world has profound consequences: If a man keeps a woman in any kind of bondage, be it physical, mental, or spiritual, he too is in bondage. Humans have suffered terribly because of this bondage. Any injustice carries its own weight of restrictions, the price of which must be paid. In this age of Spirit, all things hidden must now come into the light. The deeds done in secret are now shouted from the rooftops via our modern communication tools like television, the Internet, handheld devices, etc. No matter who we are, there is no place to hide from an omniscient God. We now must move from being a reader of God's Word to a doer. We have to apply what we have learned. This enlightenment means issues will be clearer in our minds and our hearts.

A Wrong Picture

During the funeral service for Pope John Paul II and the election of the new pope, there were no women present for the proceedings. Are they not working side by side with those important men for the same God and the same purpose? The masses of men during these events were a sight to behold. Am I alone in thinking that there was something wrong with that picture? A woman spoke up and said that she was disappointed with the election, that the new pope will follow the old traditions, which means no change, only the status quo. She said she had hoped for equality and partnership. But nothing is lost, because the Holy Spirit is the *one* who will rule the affairs of all. The pope is under His rule. He has no other choice but to follow the dictates of the Holy Spirit. This pope, as one of the leaders of Christendom, will bring in the consciousness of the kingdom of God upon earth. This is the kingdom we prayed for in the LORD's Prayer for two thousand years. That is the pope's assignment, which comes with the ability to bring men and women together, which is not an easy undertaking. This will start a new era for the Catholic Church. The new teachings of the age of Spirit are the dawning of the age of oneness, which will break down all barriers. This is not an easy assignment, but God in His mercy chose the right man for the job. He has a curious mind and is a man who likes to listen to others. He is well equipped to go with the old traditions, but by the grace of God, he will embrace this powerful new assignment. Then the proper picture will emerge.

> I thank my God every time I remember you, constantly praying with joy in every one of my prayers for all of you.
>
> Philippians 1:3-4

The coming changes to our world are giving women the opportunity to show their true nature and their nurturing spirit by taking care of, sheltering, protecting, and comforting others. To stay on the sidelines is no more our gain. Giving wings to men cannot help us on this journey of equal opportunity. It is time for violence and war to end on this planet. The sons and daughters that women brought into the world will not have to give their lives for political causes. They will experience the peace and unity that has always been their true inheritance. Women have not understood their true nature and the blessings it holds for the entire human race. True understandings of our endless opportunities will be ours. Humans are wonderfully made. We are divine beings and should be treated with utmost respect. The women who never had this understanding and denigrated their gender will embrace this truth. Yes, we need all hands on deck. Men are much more tolerant with one another; let us take a lesson from them.

Women have a way of putting themselves down while men cheer them on. The role each plays is well rehearsed. These games produce broken people and wounded souls who search and hunger for love. Many feel they will never find true love; others try, only to be disappointed over and over again. As our earth cries, so cry men, women, and children.

Men, Women, and Children

> The merciful man doeth good to his own soul,
> but he that is cruel troubleth his own flesh.
> Proverbs 11:17

We are living at a turning point in the history of mankind. Many things will change in and around us. We are in the middle of a major evolution. These changes put a great strain not only on our bodies, but also on our souls and spirits. The cleansing of the planet has already begun. Many voices have spoken about changes that are coming for us. Don't be surprised when things are done differently or in a totally new way. Let us be guided by the spirit (the voice within) on a day-to-day basis.

> And this I pray, that your love may abound yet more and more in knowledge and in all judgment; that ye may approve things that are excellent: that ye may be sincere and without offence till the day of Christ.
>
> Philippians 1:9-10

Lay a Foundation of Love

To lay a foundation of love, we have to first acknowledge that we have neglected and ignored our souls. We must become aware of what abides in our hearts and souls. We must open up our threshold of feelings that we have managed to lock up for so long. This does not include selfish reasons or the need we have for our own pleasure. It is the pure love we have in our hearts, which we will find for all of God's creation. It is a gift we give ourselves. If we believe we deserve this love of self, then respect and appreciation will come with it. In other words, the essence of our life is laid bare. So far, we have reasoned with our minds, not with our hearts. Our feelings were held down and buried somewhere inside us. We can only change and heal what we know to be true. Our emotional bodies have been in pain.

Men Do Not Show Their Feelings

Most males are taught from birth not to show their feelings or shed tears. They have become fearful of showing any kind of emotion. They are suppressing their true feelings, and they do not talk about their emotions because they have not learned how to deal with the pain. Nor do they like to be hurt by those feelings. Women tend to show their feelings and sometimes cry a lot. How many women have cried rivers of tears? The heroines suffer in silence. The female principle is equated with weakness. This is the adopted way in the Western culture.

Men are accomplished at remaining isolated from their feelings. In many cases, life has passed them by in a most twisted way. To return to the root of feelings is not easy. It takes time to reconnect. To be in touch with themselves brings them in touch with their feelings. It is a God-given gift to be a whole person. Let the male population look around and see the havoc they have caused in the world. What can a woman do with a macho image?

Through time, males have allowed important energy fields to shut down. They are controlled by their minds. This intellectual power has turned against them and made them impersonal. In this generation, they have come full circle and mostly fix their minds on the lower self. This faculty of the mind does not respect the life flow or even life itself. Of course, I am not speaking about every male. There are males who are very much in touch with their feelings.

Certain men have bragged about their accomplishments in the world. Their comprehension to build and destroy brought them a sense of achievement. Their intellect moved them to a place of disobedience and disrespect for the godly impulses. Some believe they can overrule God's ordinances. This has been done before by other civilizations, which led to detrimental outcomes.

Open the Gates to Your Feelings

Men and women's responsibilities are to regenerate their emotional bodies. Women have started this work and have come a long way. The gates must be opened to let all those good feelings flow. Being emotionally closed has brought nothing but pain to men, women, and children. Where has the true love gone that women search for in a man? What has man done to the woman who has nothing but love in her heart? How far did she go to find that love? What has she done to herself to deem herself worthy of a man's love? Women have destroyed their bodies and health. Where is the compassion women waited to find? As well, there are many children that are missing a father or mother figure in their lives. So many lives have been wrecked and are difficult to put back together again. Millions of tears were shed, while disappointments rose in women's hearts. Women have raised children by themselves, in most cases without child support or help of any kind. Many men have looked the other way, acquired a new partner, and started another family. The government itself looked away, pretending this situation would work itself out, only to find that the same men did this to other women. Women have been seeking assistance from the government, and there is no one who stops this impulsive behavior. All this was done in the name of love. Mostly men who only use their lower impulses act this way.

Some men in our time have become unsure of themselves, for the old and proven ways do not work for them anymore. Sexual unions come and go for men, which leaves them lonely and lost. They do not know where to turn or what the cause of this situation is. In desperation, they try and try again. At the end, they have much to lose, especially their power over women.

The Relationship between Man and Woman

It is no secret that many relationships between men and women have become wounded and troubled, which causes agony. Negativity plays itself out in those unions and puts a false label of dependence on it. In some cases, they lock themselves into a prison of hopelessness. As Dr. Phil says on his show, "How is this working for you?"

All humans have a female and male aspect to their beings. Women have started to work on their male side, to take back the power that is rightfully theirs. However, it is hard for some males to embrace their feminine side or show their feelings. To give up power over females is hard to do because it requires the male to stop playing his egotistical games. Manipulation and power play are a big part in those miserable relationships. Through many generations, the male has moved further and further away from the part that is love. He was mixed up with something that has nothing to do with love. Not only that, but he tried to convince women to believe the same, and many accepted it. Women know in their hearts that something is not right.

In many cases, it is no longer possible for certain men to connect their sexuality with their hearts, much less their spirituality. That is one of the reasons they fall deeper into their lower bodies. This side rules some of them with an unrelenting purpose. There are women who moved down to this level as well, especially in the younger generations.

Women Bent To Their Roles

For thousands of years there was no breathing room for women. Many women became status symbols, property, or caretakers and were reduced to being second-class citizens. Through many generations, they bent to this role. Now women rebel against this injustice. Many walk away confused and lonely, never knowing what exactly made them walk away or never knowing why this love match did not work out. Pornography and rape speak clearly about this distorted picture. It shows how low the male has fallen to misuse the creature of love beside him. Male dogmas did the rest to relegate women to an inferior status.

Since the woman is a creature of love, it is hard, at times almost impossible, for her to free herself from a relationship she imagines is made of love, but at the end, she knows what real love should be and she will walk away. Her nature is harmony and peace. She thrives in an environment where she can raise her young in a peaceful setting. She excels in the power of love to change any situation. This is the "magic" in creation. The principle of "love" is used by her and through her. Since, in many cases, those channels of love dried up, sickness, pain, and misery have come about. Feeling unloved and negative influences manifest in their children. Those parents are in most cases unable to help their children.

So many families are destroyed and torn apart, causing heartache after heartache with no help in sight. The children walk away from their parents; they see no role models in them. Many children and young adults are looking for spiritual wisdom, which is hard to find. The emptiness they experience is covered up with artificial means. Where there is no love, dark forces have easy access. The children then find comfort in the entertainment industry. They cover their pain with drugs, alcohol, and sex. Many parents and children are in the midst of a tragedy. The pain of separation from children can be severe. Part of a whole generation is lost as they go their own destructive way.

The Union of Love

The union between a man and a woman symbolizes creation energy and sets this energy free. It is a direct line to God-consciousness. It brings two people together in their own divinity. The energy of the mother principle brings the power of life. The love of a union should not be sexual only, but needs to be a flowing fountain of love, binding the hearts of both partners together. Through that union of love, one can move to higher grounds.

Love is a great mystery and allows the soul to climb higher. This truth has always been known, but it has been covered up and a false light has been put on it. Mistreatments of the worst kind are used to enslave women. Those souls have little opportunity to move higher. As such, those unions break up and disperse. Women are pushed in the opposite direction, becoming servants. Where can that take women? This condition will come to an end in our time. However, it has become deeply entrenched into women's hearts, and it will take time for them to come out of this condition. Women were not sent to earth to please men, but men and women were sent to make earth a better place together.

To step away from the fountain of love means drying out, losing life energy. Where love rules, hate and aggression will not be present. The result of this can be seen in individuals and families. The fight of the two sexes has come to an end. Victory must come for both sexes and with it, a profound understanding toward one another.

The words of love, with wisdom spoken, will flow into many hearts. Men and women will evaluate their relationships and adjust them according to their connection. Constant growth and motion of all things is taking place.

The great love stories of our time are full of tears, sorrow, and separations. There is a time for healing and that time is now. Are marital unions a bridge to understanding for both people involved, or has the union become one of comfort? Is the love still there? Is there anything left one can build on? If there is a spark of love, then work on it and bring that small flame to a roaring fire. Let us request and give our partners respect, attention, and admiration. This planet can only be healed by love. Be aware that our God will forever pour His Spirit of love upon His children. The world does not exist isolated in the universe, but it is part of a multidimensional cosmos and is bound by higher laws.

Our souls are troubled because we are trained to rely on our intellect. However, every heart longs for love. Through this love, we gain entrance to our souls. Let us examine our daily occurrences with our hearts and not with our minds. To speak from our hearts and see with our hearts is now more important than ever. We might see things on this planet in the future with our eyes that will trouble us. Again, let us look only with our hearts.

Nothing can happen to us during this turbulent time if we ask for protection from above. Let us ask for guidance and direction. Light and love are the greatest forces. The light of God is now strong on this planet. Let us take the growth of our soul very seriously, for we are caretakers of our souls. We control and check our thoughts. Let them be only positive, for they create our own reality. What we think, we become. Negative thoughts need to be changed into positive ones. Let us go on a journey of discovery to learn the universal laws. Let us see how much love we can find in our hearts. Once we discover this fact, we can set it free and let it do its own work. This is the time to listen to that small voice within.

How did we get to this point? Through generations, love was changed from what it was at the beginning until, in this generation, true love is almost unrecognizable. God said in His Word, "You have left that first love." Women have suffered greatly over time. This does not mean men have been spared. They also are part of broken families, unhappy marriages, and untold pain. Does this mean it happens to everybody? Of course not, but those who went or go through this pain know in the stillness of their hearts that something has not worked or is not working in their lives.

Our planet is sick because our souls are sick. Collectively, the pain is too much to bear for Mother Nature. Planet Earth needs healing. We are in the middle of this transformation, which will become more visible and noticeable in the future.

We will change the course of our destiny. Just like we learned to become hard, we can also relearn to get in touch with our feelings. To live a life without love is empty. Let life's joy flow freely and remember our life is a gift, knowing that our Father directs our steps.

Every soul longs for love.

From The Beginning

> The heart of her husband doth safely trust in her, so that he shall have no need of spoil.
>
> Proverbs 31:11

A Thanksgiving Feast

My spiritual mother, Beverly Marts, gave a Thanksgiving feast on February 8, 2004, for the liberation of all women in the world. The feast took place in Immokalee, Florida. Prayers were said by three sisters to celebrate God's Trinity. A brother, George Morales, gave the spiritual balance through his prayer and asked the Most High for the liberation of all mankind. A vision by Sister Beverly described a powerful light circling around each person during prayers and accomplishing its work.

Let Us Go Back To the Foundation

From the beginning, God gave his blessings to both Adam and Eve. He created male and female, blessed them, and said to them, "Be fruitful and multiply, and fill the earth, subdue it, and have dominion."

This shows clearly that the blessings were given to both equally without distinction. It is a single blessing, which is for, and available to, both of them and is applicable to the whole human race—to every man and woman during all times. Men and women are created equal and will remain so. This can never change; there can be no separation or division. God loves each facet of Himself equally.

Every Offspring Comes Through the Womb of a Woman

God told us to be fruitful, which means to have children.

Every child comes through the womb of a woman. This blessing can never be exhausted, because this source is inexhaustible and remains a source of man's continuing procreation. To fill the earth is a purpose and also the aim of the blessings. Numbers are not important. The fullness of the earth implies first harmony, fellowship, and unity. The ultimate goal, although we choose to reach it through hardships, divisions, strife, and wars, is to regain the relationship we had with God in the beginning.

There is a father and a mother aspect to God. God, our Father, has a fatherly and a motherly love within Him. By creating Adam and Eve in the beginning, He made them in His image, which is both male and female. Eve's love was not strong enough to withstand temptation. When Lucifer tempted her, she fell under his power. She, in turn, tempted Adam, who lost his position with God. As a result, God's plan changed. This is the time for all mysteries that had once been hidden from ages and generations to be revealed (Colossians 1:26).

Satan Tempted Eve

We have been taught that Eve took an apple from the forbidden tree of life and gave it to Adam. The Bible speaks of a tree in the garden and the fruit thereof. Satan tempted her to taste the fruit and said to her, "Your eyes shall be opened, and you shall be as God, knowing good and evil." He beguiled her and pulled her into his game. Once he had united with her, his job was done. She then begged Adam to do the same with her.

Satan used sex to bring the human race down to his level. From that time on, Adam and Eve, who had walked and talked with God, could not see or hear Him anymore. Adam had one last conversation with God, but only after God asked him, "Where are thou?" He admitted to God that it was the woman who gave him the fruit from the tree and he did eat. King David cried out in Psalms 51:5, "In sin did my mother conceive me." This is the original sin that all generations are under.

In this end time, Satan again is trying to destroy this world through immorality. Sex is used to destroy this generation. He has tried and succeeded to involve men and women again in the same game. Humans are participating in an unprecedented level of sexual permissiveness that has degraded women and men. Even very young girls think they must look sexy for men.

> Do they not err that devise evil? But mercy and truth shall be to them that devise good.
>
> Proverbs 14:22

> Adam called his wife Eve; because she was the mother of all living.
>
> Genesis 3:20.

Have we forgotten what Adam and Eve had in the garden of Eden? They walked and talked with God. This generation will do the same again. God told us in the Revelation 21:3 that He will dwell with us and be our God again. In spite of our different characteristics and peculiarities, this God has commanded us *to love one another*. This one commandment, given to us two thousand years ago by the gentle man from Galilee, will lead us back to the oneness that is our heritage. That commandment must now be practiced on our planet and makes the Ten Commandments obsolete, because it encompasses their teachings. In this new era of the Spirit, this will be the law for all mankind. Anybody who contravenes this law will be arrested spiritually. This law will also affect those who do not know it, because the opportunity to learn and hear about it was provided.

Whenever we are interacting with another person, we are interacting with God. When we do something good to someone, we are doing good to God. However, if we do something bad, we are also doing it to God.

There Is No Divided Authority

We cannot divide the authority of men and women. This is impossible, for it is a comprehensive understanding of all human life. The contributions that will bring true results will come from the duality of men and women. To have dominium over the earth as it was given to us at the beginning makes us realize that we are all stewards of it. To be stewards does not give us the right to kill any living being, but we should protect and take care of all creatures; they also have a right to live. To be in the perfect circle that God enjoys with all of His creation, we cannot, in the age of wisdom and understanding, kill as we see fit.

> Behold, I have given you every herb bearing seed, which is upon the face of all the earth, and every tree, in the which is the fruit of a tree yielding seed; to you it shall be for meat.
>
> Genesis 1:29

This ordinance has never been changed even though we took things into our own hands. We say we have to kill in order to eat. Not any more. God has heard the cry of the animals. He will change things for them and give humans the understanding to respect and love His creation.

Men and Women Must Work Together

If a man places obstacles before his female counterpart, he places that obstacle in his own path. Then his own efforts are stifled and dissipated by his own actions. God gave blessings to mankind on the condition that men and women work together in unity toward one single goal of making the world a better place. This must be a combined action. Men tend to rule the world with their heads, while women rule with their hearts. In this age, they must become one heart and one mind. Hearts are to rule over minds. Only through joint efforts can the city of God be built.

Women Must Be Given Their Rightful Places

Men have not accomplished their goals because they have not given women their rightful place upon this earth. In many cases, women have not been recognized for their contributions. Men have turned women from a natural into an unnatural state. Men have forgotten to look into their hearts; they looked on the outside to satisfy their lust. Some women try so hard to satisfy the male eyes and wants. This has brought both sexes much pain and suffering. Many women have allowed themselves to be made into lesser beings by men and are used by them for their satisfaction. Women accepted this lowering, and it will take time to regain the rightful place God intended them to have.

The imbalance between males and females started a long time ago. Men and women used to divide tasks. Men were hunter/gatherers, while women tended to the meals, the clothing, the dwellings, and the children. Men became powerful, while women became subjugated. Men began depriving women of equality, of which more was lost with each passing generation. Many men blame women consciously or subconsciously for the loss of the garden of Eden. The existence of women's rights vanished for a time on this earth to be rediscovered in this generation.

> And Cain knew his wife, and she conceived and bore Enoch; and he built a city and named it after the name of his son, Enoch.
>
> Genesis 4:17

The work of a woman is to teach her children the spiritual, as well as the human, laws. The spiritual teachings do not cancel out the importance of an earthly education. There must be balance between human and spiritual knowledge. We now have the task to build an eternal everlasting city.

We Are God's Cities

During human civilizations, how many cities have been built and destroyed? Men and women who build a temple within themselves, where God abides day and night, construct the eternal city that is to come. We are God's buildings. We are His cities, which can never be destroyed. Until now, we have struggled blindly through darkness and lawlessness.

Many know the story of the tower of Babel in Genesis 11:4, which is a great illustration of man's physical journey on earth. They tried to fulfill their greatest ambitions and paid no heed to their maker or the spiritual element. They said to one another: "Come, let us build ourselves a city and a tower that reaches into the heavens, and let us make a name for ourselves, lest we be scattered upon the face of the earth. How many times have we tried and succeeded to make a name for ourselves?

This story describes an unsuccessful attempt by man. This generation has also perfected such practices. In reality, God only lets us go as far as He wants us to go. In Babel, they planned to immortalize themselves and bring themselves to the heavens with their towering construction. Are we not doing the same today? Are we not trying and searching to immortalize ourselves? Their hearts were not turned towards their Father, nor are ours. We fumble around in darkness instead of turning to the master planner for some much-needed illumination. All our modern-day constructions, our high-rise buildings, and our aims to go to the moon and other planets provide evidence that man's heart still wants to accomplish his ambitions. During all times, humans have ignored their maker. We developed the art of going around Him. There are many people in the world today who make a name for themselves and who ignore the plight of those who suffer. Humankind has not managed to bring security to this planet. All money belongs to God. Therefore, we have a great opportunity to make a name for ourselves in heavenly places. Good deeds are recorded in higher places.

We Are Moving Toward Peace

Men and women are moving toward peace in spite of the violence and struggles that are prevalent in the world. We are moving toward stability; it is the way to eternal life. To subdue the world implies a certain struggle by the human race to overcome hostile forces, be they natural or man-made. However, this can easily be accomplished by an enlightened race. This task is laid upon men and women, without partiality, to be accomplished in this time.

Women of Old Show Us the Way

Strength and honor are her clothing; and she shall rejoice in the time to come.

Proverbs 31:25

Women Were Always Equal Before God

Since the beginning of time, women were equal in the eyes of God, who created them. It was the Almighty Himself who gave Adam a companion. From that time on, women became the tunnel through which every human being comes to planet earth. God Himself chose this channel when He came to earth. Angels with long-term assignments, as well as prophets, must all come through a woman. Because of this great assignment God gave women, they must be respected at all times. Adam and Eve, God's first human creations, came with a clear distinction between male and female, for both sexes were expressing the image of God.

Eve was the first woman and the mother of the whole world. Through Eve and then Adam, we lost the kingdom; it will be regained in this time. Eve's role and choices were described in an earlier chapter. We will examine how the women in the Bible did things in their days and how they played a role in the history of mankind. Those women were remarkable and are still examples in our time. Through their faith, they accomplished great feats with astonishing endurance.

They survived not only political, but also economical restrictions and triumphed in carrying their crosses. Those women of God left a legacy for us. Tears and joys, laughter and despair shine through in their stories. Women of great faith can be found from the beginning up to now. The pages of yesteryear give glimpses of courage and show the gentleness of strong women. The spirit and influence of those women can still be felt. Their lives can be roadmaps for us that may lead us on and upward.

The cultural and historical settings may change, yet their inspirations and their triumphs stay with us. In those days, the world was more difficult for women than in our time. Our foremothers' main purpose was to tend to their husbands, bear children, and raise them. They were to run everything smoothly. If their husbands mistreated them, it was their lot in life; there was nothing they could do.

Let the reader's imagination see those women in a light that will help understand ourselves. Proverbs 31:25 tells us that women will laugh in the coming times. We are now laughing; the promise is coming to pass. Thank you, Father.

In the Old Testament, we meet a woman named Sarah, whom I loved from the first time I heard her story. Of course, when talking about Sarah, her husband Abraham must be included also. To follow God's call, they traveled thousands of miles. Their journey from Ur to Haran in Egypt and back to the land of Canaan was long and arduous. The hot, dry sands of those desert lands buried evidence of pots, vases, temples, and public places, which are being rediscovered in modern times.

God's call came to Abraham early on. Hebrews 11:8 tells us he left his own country not knowing where he would go. When Abraham was seventy-five years old, he again was summoned by one of God's calls. To prepare for a long journey was not an easy task. Searching for water in the desert for hundreds of people and livestock was a troublesome job. They had to avoid raiding bands of nomads; survival was a daily challenge.

Sarah Means "Princess"

> And I will bless her, and give thee a son also of her: yea, I will bless her, and she shall be a mother of nations; kings of people shall be of her.
>
> Genesis 17:16

Sarah was attracted to Abraham when she was very young, and he was in love with her from the first time he saw her. Abraham made sure that Sarah was well taken care of once she was married to him. She enjoyed money, position, influence, and servants because her husband was prosperous. However, Sarah was barren, which left an empty spot in Abraham's heart. Children meant immortality for a husband in those days. Sarah lived in a man's world. Abraham was aware that Sarah had left a lot behind to marry him. She came from the city of Ur, of the Chaldeans, a center of culture, philosophy, and astronomy, but she chose to live in the desert and in tents with him.

They adopted Abraham's nephew, Lot. After growing up, Lot left to live in the city of Sodom, and Abraham became very lonely. When Lot was held hostage, Abraham went to war against his captors. After Lot was freed, Abraham met a man who had stopped his caravan and asked him to kneel down so that he could bless him. Abraham was surprised but did as he was told. He recognized that it was King Melchizedek, whose name meant "king of righteousness," and he gave him ten percent of everything he had. Sarah did not meet King Melchizedek on this occasion.

A few years later, this same man came with two companions (angels) to their tent one afternoon. Abraham greeted them heartily and pleaded with them to stay for a meal. Sarah was called to help serve the men. She was excited to meet this man, for she had heard so much about him. He told her that she would have a son. Sarah laughed, for she was old by now. He asked her, "Is anything too hard for the LORD?" She admitted that it was not.

Sarah waited and waited, but year after year, there was no issue. She was a woman of faith, but it took too long for her. In desperation, she asked Abraham to lay with their maid, Hagar. He obeyed her and Hagar bore a son for Abraham. They named him Ishmael. Hagar and Sarah did not get along. There was contempt and jealousy between them. Sarah insisted on sending Hagar and her son away. Abraham was grief-stricken over this, but it was God's intention that they leave. Fourteen years passed with Ishmael being their only son.

God's promises became reality when Sarah became pregnant at an old age and delivered the son of promise called "Isaac." His name meant "laughter." The grief of all those years of not being a mother gave way to joy over this gift from God. Sarah was described as a beautiful woman. Kings asked for her attention. Nowhere else does the Bible state that a woman was fair to look at. Sarah was not perfect but did what needed to be done. She was a woman who accepted new possibilities and who was in tune with life. She accepted her cross proudly and with long-suffering.

Rebekah Changed the Course of History

> And Isaac brought her into his mother Sarah's tent, and took Rebekah, and she became his

wife; and he loved her; and Isaac was comforted after his mother's death.

Genesis 24:67

Rebekah was a woman who changed the course of history. She was a woman of decisiveness and was without hesitation. Her strength and certainty was found in her words, "I will go," when she was asked if she would go with strangers to marry in a faraway land. This describes her well, because if something needed to be done, she was ready to do it. Once she made up her mind, she followed through with actions. When she pushed her younger son into a lie, he feared being discovered, but she replied, "Upon me be your curse, my son; only obey my word and go" (Genesis 27:13).

When Isaac, the promised son of Abraham and Sarah, was forty years old, his father decided it was time for him to take a wife. A trusted servant was sent to Haran, the city of Nahor, to find a wife for him. Once the servant arrived, he made sure he would be at the well where young women picked up their water supply at a certain time of the day. The servant prayed first to God to show him the right woman. As Rebekah stopped at the well, he stepped forward to ask her for some water for himself and the camels. She agreed willingly, so he knew it was a sign from above that she was the one. He told her of Abraham and Isaac; she discovered that they were family.

The servant was invited to her house for an evening meal. But before he would eat, he told of his intention of finding a wife for Isaac and that God had given him a sign when he saw Rebekah. Her parents listened politely and asked her what she wanted to do. "I will go," was her simple and firm answer (Genesis 24:58). She took nothing with her but her beloved maid, Deborah. The journey away from home lasted many days. Once they came close to the estate, she saw Isaac in the fields. She covered her face with a veil and greeted him. He took her to his mother's tent. He loved her from the first time he saw her (Genesis 24:67).

> So they called Rebekah and asked her, will you go with this man?
>
> Genesis 24:58

Rebekah was also the forerunner of all women who left their homes and traveled to foreign countries with men they barely knew and to an unknown future, putting their trust in God and having faith in Him. Many of them suffered disappointments and hardships. Others found great marriages and a new life.

Isaac and Rebekah

The wedding was celebrated happily. Fifteen years passed and Rebekah was still without child. They prayed for a child, and the Lord heard them. Rebekah became pregnant, but from the beginning, there was trouble inside her womb. She went to the Lord to inquire about it. He said to her in Genesis 25:23,

> Two nations are in thy womb, and two manners of people shall be separated from thy bowels: and the one people shall be stronger than the other people: and the elder shall serve the younger.

Two nations came from her womb. Who were those two nations? Two different characteristics came from her bowels. One son (or one nation) would be stronger than the other. The elder son would serve the younger one. This was a strange statement, for in those days, the elder always inherited the estate. Who are those two nations? Rebekah had twins, Esau was red and hairy (black), the other was smooth and fair (white) and was named Jacob. Esau's name was later changed to Edom and Jacob's to Israel. While Esau, the older, was his father's favorite and a hunter like him, the younger was his mother's favorite and stayed in the tents with her. The boys grew into manhood and the days of deceit arrived.

The first incident happened when Esau came home from hunting. He was so hungry, he was about to faint. He called his brother Jacob to quickly bring him something to eat. His brother insisted he would feed him only if Esau would give him his birthright in exchange. In desperation, Esau agreed to it and as a consequence, he lost his birthright as the elder son.

The next incident changed everything for the human race and laid the foundation for things to come. Who was behind it? Rebekah. When Isaac, their father, realized that he was near death, he asked his beloved son, Esau, to go and hunt his favorite game. "Fix it for me the way I like it, so that I may bless you," he said. Rebekah overheard this conversation and wanted Jacob to receive the blessing. She went to the kitchen, fixed Isaac's favorite food, and had Jacob bring it to his father. The Bible says Isaac, who was blind by then, discerned him not and blessed him.

> Therefore God give thee of the dew of heaven, and the fatness of the earth, and plenty of corn and wine. Let people serve thee, and nations bow down to thee: be LORD over thy brethren, And let thy mother's sons bow down to thee. Cursed be everyone that curseth thee, and blessed be he that blessed thee.
>
> Genesis 27:28-29

Through this blessing, the descendants of Jacob (the white race) were blessed, while the descendants of Esau (the black race) had to suffer because of his father's words. One woman's decision changed the course of history. Which nation and people are very blessed? Which nation has been cheated out of the blessings that were rightfully their inheritance? Understandably, when Esau came home and discovered this cruel turn of events, he cried bitterly and asked his father for a blessing. Isaac's blessing for Esau:

> Behold, thy dwelling shall be the fatness of the earth, and of the dew of heaven from above;

> and by thy sword shall thou live, and shall serve thy brother; and it shall come to pass when thou shall have the dominion, that thou shall break his yoke from off thy neck.
>
> Genesis 27:39-40

These fateful words are being fulfilled in our time. The yoke is taken off the black man's neck now.

When Rebekah heard that Esau planned revenge against his brother Jacob, she asked her younger son to go to her native country so that Esau would not harm him. On that fateful day, Rebekah lost both her sons; she became tired of her life and died soon after. When Deborah, her maid, had passed away, Rebekah planted a special oak tree by her grave, which was called the "tree of weeping."

Rebekah started a course of action that changed the whole world. She did not wait for God to fulfill His promises. The young girl at the well changed so much. She came a long way to fulfill her destiny. A strong woman emerged who was chosen by God for His plan. Her independent decision was God's will.

Bathsheba, the Lover of King David

> And when the mourning was past, David sent and brought her to his house, and she became his wife, and bare him a son. But the thing that David had done displeased the Lord.
>
> 2 Samuel 11:27

All we know about Bathsheba is that King David summoned her after he had watched this lovely girl take a bath on a rooftop. Of course, there was more to this story, which has all the ingredients of a movie. We find love, lust, seduction, and murder. It was said that King David's men who picked her up, "took her" (2 Samuel 11:4).

She had no choice in this matter, no time to weigh the consequences. Truly, it was a no-win situation because she was a married woman who had to follow her king's orders. The most powerful man in that part of the country wanted her—the king! Could she simply have said, "No, I am not going?" Her husband was away at war. She could have lost her life if she had refused King David's request. She became pregnant immediately, which brought about another problem. The Hebrew law said, "If a man commits adultery with the wife of his neighbor, both the adulterer and the adulteress shall be put to death" (Leviticus 20:10).

More problems arose when King David brought Uriah, her husband, back from battle so he could sleep with his wife to cover up the pregnancy. However, the requirements were that a soldier practice abstinence from sexual relations while on military leave. Bathsheba must have had heard that her husband had returned from battle. Was she waiting for him during the night? Would he come home to her? Or did she look out the door in fear? Did she feel lonely and isolated?

Uriah would not sleep with his wife. King David's scheme did not work. Even after Uriah was made drunk, he did not come close to his wife. King David then gave orders to put him in the fiercest battle and leave him unprotected so he would be killed.

Did Bathsheba know about this? Once she heard that her husband was dead, she lamented for him (2 Samuel 11:26). As it was, King David married Bathsheba after her husband's death. Their first son died; they both grieved for a long time (2 Samuel 12:24). However, they lived to see how their second son, Solomon, was given the throne of Israel over King David's first legitimate son (1 Kings 1:28-31).

King David was a man who loved God. He showed reverence for the ark of God; and he loved music and poetry, but his love for Bathsheba led him to murder and to his downfall. He was a man who had many wives and many concubines, yet he insisted on having another man's only wife. We do not know much of Bathsheba's early years with the king. She probably had to deal with his ample harem. Her intelligence, wisdom, and beauty gave her influence in the court. Soon he was an old man, but she stayed strong and vigorous.

The struggle for his throne began. Bathsheba remembered a promise the king had made to her earlier. He had told her that their son, Solomon, would someday be king. Even the old prophet, Nathan, told her to go to the king's bedroom to use her influence in this matter. The dying king listened carefully and gave her what she wanted (1 Kings 1:16-21).

Bathsheba went from a frightened woman who was forced to have sex with the king to a person of prestige and influence. Her life seemed to change in an instant. There are many "Bathsheba's" in the world who are victims of lust, rape, and brutality. The hardships of wars have mothers grieving for their children who are dying in their arms of hunger and despair. Many become refugees. Yet they are survivors; they go on living and making the best of their lives. They become strong and overcome obstacles.

Miriam, the Sister of Moses

> His sister stood at a distance to see what would happen to him.
>
> Exodus 2:4

For three hundred years, the Hebrews were oppressed in the land of Egypt. We know from ancient scrolls, biblical accounts, and archeology that the Hebrews were wealthy and had great power. Hollywood made the movie *Exodus*, which was based on the time during the reign of Pharaoh Ramses II. Its story tells how Moses led his people out of Egypt. Little is told of the role of his sister, Miriam, who, like him, was born into a family of Jewish slaves. Early on, she learned how to overcome and survive. She helped with the plan to hide her baby brother from the slaughter of all first-born male children. She was taking the child to the river where she was to place him in a basket made lovingly by his mother. The mother's plan was to float the child near where the princess bathed daily with her servants. She had prayed that one of the women would take pity on him and protect him.

A soothsayer had warned the Pharaoh that a first-born male child of the Jewish slaves would grow more powerful than he was and would take his place as ruler of Egypt. A decree went out ordering that every first male child born to a Jewish family be killed. Cries and sobs of anguish were heard in every home in the city as the soldiers carried out this heinous act.

As planned, the princess found the child Moses. Miriam, who hid in the bushes, observed the gentle spirit of the princess. She stepped forward, knowing her brother had been saved, and offered to be the caregiver for this child. The princess accepted and brought both of them back to the palace. The Pharaoh loved this child more than his own son.

Moses grew strong and was educated along with the prince of the royal family. Moses became Pharaoh's favorite, who treated him as one of his own. Miriam did not marry so that she could be near Moses and could tell him of his birth, his heritage, and how he had become the Pharaoh's favorite.

What kind of woman was Miriam? She was a woman who made a great sacrifice to save her baby brother's life. She protected her family by taking the child from the home and exposing herself, not knowing how her mother's plan would unfold. Miriam was a prophetess and a deaconess. Later in life, she became horribly disfigured by leprosy. Lepers at that time were banished to caves far from their families. Her brothers remembered the kindness of their sister and went to visit her in the leper's caves. They brought her food and clothing, which she shared with those around her. She was known as a kind woman, yet she died alone at Kadesh.

Women of ancient times suffered greatly.

Mary, Our Example

> And she brought forth her first born son, and wrapped him in swaddling clothes and laid him in a manger because there was no room in the inn.
>
> Luke 2:7

Mary, the Mother of Jesus

Mary's parents, Anna and Joachim, had their child late in life. She was looked upon as a gift from God, for they had prayed for a long time to have a child. Before Mary was born, her parents promised God to raise her in the temple where her education and service started at a young age. She was taken care of by one of the sisters living there.

As she grew older, she was taught by the priests at the temple and listened to many of their sermons. She recognized and understood that the whole of Israel was waiting for the Savior, much like in our day. Some waited for Him to come from the clouds, just as some do today. The priests in the temple went strictly by the revelation of Mica 5:2 that Bethlehem will be the city where the ruler of Israel will come from. They waited patiently for Him to be born. Our generation is looking to Revelation 12:5, which states that a woman will deliver a male child who will rule all nations with a rod of iron. Again, some in our time wait for Him to come from the clouds.

When Mary heard the message of a child being born, she was very excited and prayed to God to let her attend to such a holy child. The Almighty had different plans for Mary. It was customary for young people to leave the temple at age fourteen or fifteen when their years of instruction were over. During that time, there was a celebration for maidens to be chosen by men to become their wives. Mary was still there for the celebration, because her parents had not yet arrived.

Joseph, a carpenter, traveled through that part of the country because of a job. He was a very serious man who had never married. As he stopped to watch the celebration, a dove landed on him. The custom at that time dictated that once a dove landed on a male, he was to be picked as a husband for a young woman. Mary was next in line for a husband. This was looked upon as a divine union. Joseph was not prepared or ready to take a wife, but as the custom demanded, he had to take the young girl, Mary, with him.

Not long after, he could see that Mary was with child. Since he knew he had not been with her, he suspected another man. He was ready to take her home to her parents. He did not plan to shame her or question her. The night before their departure, he had a dream that he should not send Mary away. It was agreed that Mary should visit her cousin, Elisabeth, in the hill country of Judea. Elisabeth herself was with child late in her life. Once Mary greeted her, Elisabeth's child leapt in her womb, and Elisabeth was filled with the Holy Spirit.

Mary, the Handmaid of God

Was Mary fearful when the angel named Gabriel visited her? From a young age on, she was surrounded by dreams, visions, and appearances of heavenly hosts. The angel said to her, "Hail thou that are highly favored, the LORD is with thee: Blessed art thou among women." Mary was troubled after hearing this. The angel told her not to be afraid, that she had found favor with God and would bear a son, whom she was to call Jesus. Mary wondered how this could be, since she did not know a man. The angel answered, "The Holy Ghost shall come upon thee and the power of the Highest shall overshadow thee." Her answer was, "Behold the handmaid of the LORD, be it unto me according to thy word" (Luke 1:28–38). Mary had understood that she was to be a servant of God.

Her Son was born and put in a manger surrounded by animals. Did she think about the things that happened to her? Did she question certain things daily? We don't know. Life has its on way of dealing with problems. But all through the years Jesus grew up, Mary had confirmations that this child she delivered was different.

Mary and Joseph's Revelations

When Jesus was seven days old, Mary and Joseph took Him to the temple for the traditional child blessing. An old prophet, Simeon, had been waiting for this day. He prayed that he should not die before he saw this child. As he took the child into his arms, he prophesied that this child would be a light unto the gentiles and a glory for his people, Israel. Mary and Joseph marveled at his sayings. He also gave a revelation to Mary. "A sword shall pierce through thy soul," he told her. Mary could only imagine the things that were to come.

Jesus grew in wisdom and stature. When He was twelve years old, during the yearly visit to the temple, He stayed back without letting his parents know where He was. Mary and Joseph were anxious with worry and had to go back a day's journey to find him. He was in the temple talking to the doctors of law and answering their questions. When Mary asked Him why He worried his parents so much, he replied, "I must be about my Father's business" (Luke 2:46-49).

The time came for Jesus to start His ministry. Did Mary know where it would lead Him? At the wedding at Canaan, she asked Him to change water into wine. He said to her, "Woman, my hour has not yet come." However, He fulfilled her request. When the time of sorrow came, Mary was following her son to Calvary. He knew his mother was there, for He said to John, "Behold, your mother."

Mary Is Blessed By All Generations

Her story is remembered each Christmas by most. For others, she is merely an alabaster figure. Mary is the most revered female in Christianity. She is the best-known woman in the Bible and is very real to women. She shows us the blessings a woman can receive from God and how obedience can carry us through assignments. She is the one person who rectified the sin Eve brought upon us. Mary's son, our LORD Jesus Christ, took our sins away (Romans 5:19). By one man's disobedience, we were made sinners; by one man's obedience, we are made righteous.

Mary is exalted because of her astonishing assignment, which was not an easy one. She was a young girl who found herself pregnant. She put her trust completely in God and was richly rewarded for it. God, in his infinite wisdom, gave her the much-needed companionship of her older cousin Elisabeth, who brought forth John the Baptist. They had much in common and became inseparable for a time. Their dependency on God and each other is a great example of sisterhood in action.

Through Mary's obedience, the history of salvation for all mankind begins. Mary glorified a God who uses whom He likes to accomplish His plans, man or woman, the downtrodden, the powerless, and those who are counted as nothing in the world.

> God has chosen the foolish things of the world to confound the wise; and God has chosen the weak things of the world to confound things which are mighty.
>
> 1 Corinthians 1:27

Mary Teaches All Women

Mary's life journey was fraught with pain and tears. It was a life of service. She was led by God's will. She did not murmur or walk away from bearing her cross. Whenever the Holy Spirit has an assignment for us, we should do our best to fulfill it. Mary, the mother of Jesus, is an example of how to do the will of God. She has set all of us free through the birth of our Savior. She undid Eve's wrongdoing in the garden of Eden.

Now the Holy Spirit challenges us to live a Christlike life and grow in the power of His essence to fulfill our destinies. No matter what comes our way, we should always give thanks to God. The spirit of prophecy will fill us the way it did in Mary's time. God will open our eyes and make us understand what an impact the Holy Spirit has on us. Truly, we will become new creatures in Christ.

Martha, Mary, and Lazarus: Friends of Jesus

> Jesus loved Martha and her sister and Lazarus.
>
> John 11:5

Martha, Mary, and Lazarus were like family to the Christ. He enjoyed coming to their house, where He found a warm, hearty welcome. The house was in Bethany, about two miles from Jerusalem. The families visited often before He started His ministry. The loving relationship that he shared with them sustained Him during his public years. One day He received a message from Martha to come quickly, for her brother was very sick. When Christ got the message, He said that Lazarus's sickness was not unto death, but for the glory of God. By the time He arrived, Lazarus had been dead for days. Martha had been anxious for Him to come. She even went down the street to meet Him. When she finally confronted Him, she was so disturbed, she blurted out that her brother would not have died if He had been there on time. When Christ told her that her brother would rise from death, she had to think for a while. She was a woman of faith and thought it must be after his resurrection, and she told the Christ so.

Martha ran the household smoothly and was in control most of the time. But this day was a day of total disorder. The house was full of people who had come to grieve with the family. Her attention was needed to manage the funeral arrangements, prepare the food, and attend to her guests. Everybody was weeping and wailing. She called her sister Mary to her side to tell her that the Master had arrived. She was almost afraid to tell her, for she knew how much Mary loved Jesus. Right now, she needed her sister at her side, not at her Master's feet. But to her dismay, Mary was by His side again and was listening to His words, which were sheer joy for her.

Christ commanded the stone be taken away from Lazarus's tomb. Martha cautioned him that by now, her brother had been dead for four days. Christ lifted up His eyes and thanked His Father who heard Him always. With a strong voice, He called out to Lazarus to come out. As the crowd watched, Lazarus was raised from the dead for all to see. Some of the Jews were amazed, yet some murmured against Jesus.

As tears turned to joy, a celebration started and Martha was trying to accommodate everybody. Again, her sister was by the Master's feet, listening to every word He was saying. She needed Mary's help. She went to the LORD and said to Him, "Can you not see that my sister has left me to serve alone? Tell her to help me." The LORD answered, "Martha, Martha, you are so concerned about many things. Mary has chosen the good part, which shall not be taken away from her."

One can see the familiarity of the Christ with this family. Otherwise, Martha would not have asked Him to tell Mary to help her (Luke 10:40). John 11:5 tells us that Jesus loved Martha, her sister, Mary, and their brother, Lazarus. Christ was like a brother to them.

Martha was not the kind of person who pretended that everything was all right when it was not. She did not hold back, hence her statement that her brother would be alive if He would have come sooner. When she was told the Christ was coming, she was not one to wait in the house, but she ran toward Him. She knew the power of this man, and so did her sister, Mary (John 11:22). She was aware of His actions.

Mary chose the spiritual path, which could not be taken away from her. Martha chose the world's ways and its traditions, which would pass away. In today's society, women choose to raise a family and to have a career. Few choose God's work, which can never be taken away from them. In the new era that we now experience, women will have a choice to have a family only or serve God and have a family as well; we will let our souls guide us. We will not go blindly into an adventure, but we will be ever mindful to fulfill our assignments, which were laid out for us before we were born.

Women during the Time of Christ

> There were also women looking on afar off; among whom was Mary Magdalene, and Mary the mother of James the less and of Joses, and Salome.
>
> Mark 15:40

Women Who Stood Under The Cross

During the first century, Judea was part of the Roman Empire. Around the year AD 30, when the Jews celebrated Passover, a passion arose for a prophet called Jesus the Christ. His popularity increased as thousands of pilgrims came to the city of Jerusalem for the celebration. Crowds cheered and went so far as to proclaim Him the Messiah. People at that time were waiting and hungry for liberation and deliverance from the plight of the Roman occupation. Many fierce religious disputes went on in the city. They felt the time was right for a prophet to arrive. Once He was in their midst, the established clergy turned quickly against Him, but some of the population followed Him, especially twelve men. A number of women were also seen with Him, which, at that time, was out of the ordinary. Jesus was born when the time had fully come (Galatians 4:4). There was temporary peace in the nation, missionary travel was allowed, and many understood the language of the Old Testament. A heightened expectancy of things to come filled the air. Christ's message was for men and women. He regarded women as equals. Women were not only created for motherhood, but also for discipleship. His actions and words spoke of a change for women. One man changed everything.

The Wind of Freedom

A wind of freedom came for women during the time of Christ. His treatment of women disturbed many, including the disciples. Jewish customs shut women off from the outer world. They had to be submissive to fathers and husbands. Their religion treated them as inferior.

Many committed women, as well as the ruling class, accompanied Christ through the cities and towns. There was Mary Magdalena, who was healed from seven demons, Joanna, the wife of Chula, who was Herod's steward, Susana, and many others who were right beside Christ as He preached the good news of the kingdom. At His crucifixion, mostly women stood in the vicinity, grieving for Him in His final hour. Most male followers had fled.

Women in those days witnessed how short life could be, how easily hope could be destroyed, and how a great message could be taken away so quickly. They had a great love for this prophet, who was like one of them. At the end, the light left their eyes. Their dreams were shattered; their hope was gone. A cold wind blew and left them shaken. Their mission was taken away from them. For a time, a giant had been in their midst who told them they could do the same work. In fact, He said, "Greater works will you do, for I go to my Father." His death showed them their limitations, their angst for things to come. In that hour, they understood sorrow and death. They saw Christ going through the human experience by suffering, by the pain of being rejected, by being sold out by a friend, and by the harassment from the clergy. Finally, He had to face shame, defeat, despair, and death—all within a few days.

Women Went To the Grave of the Master

On that dark Sunday, the women went very early to the grave of their beloved Master. It had been dark since Thursday. The betrayal of Peter's denial was still fresh on their minds. The pulling back of the disciples was another disappointment for them. The darkness of Satan's glee could almost be felt, but it was the anguish of Christ that brought them to tears when the final hour for Him had come. During the crucifixion, Christ knew the women were there. He could hear their voices. He could see their worried faces. They called out His name and whispered words of hope to Him. They had followed Him all the way up the mountain on that fateful day. Out of love and concern, they stayed with Him until His last breath. Their nurturing spirits saw them through this ordeal. After He passed, they brought ointments and spices for His lifeless body and linens to cover Him properly. They washed the blood from Him, touching His face one last time. The last ones to leave Calvary that dark day were the women in Christ's life. They were also the first to come to His grave.

Early Sunday morning they were ready for the last somber tasks. The idea that they would find an empty tomb was not on their mind. It was not fear that led them to His tomb, but duty and devotion. The task of anointing Him once more was at hand. The dreams they had were gone; their moods were somber that morning. It was all too late. Their LORD was gone. Nails now pierced the feet that had walked on water. The hands that had healed lepers and the sick were lifeless. The voice that had talked of a kingdom of love and peace was still. All they could do was put warm oil on a cold body to bid farewell to the gentle man from Galilee, who talked to them about a better time and a future of loving one another. He taught them to forgive and to give without asking for anything in return, which was a noble motivation at that time and still is.

When Your Road Becomes Dark

What if they had given up? It was the Father who looked out for his Son. He saw the women's hearts at that moment. An angel was sent to remove the stone from the grave (Matthew 28:2-3). That stone was moved for all of us. The stone that was on our hearts is gone.

The sun is on the horizon, even though it has taken two thousand more years to come to pass. When our road becomes dark and muddy, when our nights become too long, when our trail is never ending, let us not give up, let us not quit, and let us not stop. There is an angel sent our way to roll away the stone that is on our hearts. God moves in mysterious ways. He is the God of reconstruction. He hears the cry of His children. He sees the oppression of His daughters and all His children. We come out of bondage into a great light. Let us hold hands and walk to the open tomb—it is the shrine of greatness. It is the very place prepared by our God for His children. He waited a long time for us to return to Him, to the place of everlasting peace. Our Father is the great restorer of the human race, the conqueror of death and Hades. We will move away from worshipping heroes and the fame of a worldly star. Running after money and material things will become a thing of the past.

Christ Was Very Open In Forgiving Women

Some of the women following Him were very sinful. We remember the woman caught in adultery. He protected her from her accusers (John 8:7-11). He said, "He that is without sin among you, let him cast the first stone." In verse 8, Christ stooped down and wrote something on the ground. The Word of God does not reveal what He wrote in the dust, but we know that her accusers left one by one. Now we know that the words written were the sins of each individual who was present. They had no other choice but to leave in disgrace. However, the Christ gave her a valuable message by saying, "Go and sin no more." This message is for all of us, for all times.

The Woman of Samaria

John 4:7-14 describes a Samaritan woman who met the Christ at the water well. She was surprised that He would speak to a Samaritan woman, for she said, "A Jew has no dealings with us." But He explained to her that if she knew who asked her for water, she would ask Him for the living water. She was quick to ask for this special water. Christ told her to call her husband to come to this place. She replied that she had no husband. He reminded her that she had had five husbands and that the one she was with was not her husband. This made her suspicious, and she carefully mentioned that she knew that the Messiah would come who would be called the Christ (verse 25). He replied, "I that speak unto thee is He" (verse 26). He can meet us at any time in any form.

The Woman with the Alabaster Box

In Luke 7:36-38 we hear of a woman who was a sinner. When she heard that the Christ was invited to a Pharisee's house for dinner, she went there with an alabaster box of ointments. She went directly to Him and started weeping. She washed His feet with her tears and dried them with her long hair. She anointed His feet with her ointments. When the owner of the house who was an upholder of the law saw this scene, he said to himself, "If this man were a prophet, he would know that this woman is a sinner." Christ addressed him and gave him a parable. He spoke of a certain creditor who had two debtors; one owed him five hundred talents, while the other owed him only fifty. Neither could pay back the money, so he forgave them their debts. Christ asked, "Which of the two is more thankful?" Simon the Pharisee had to admit that it was the one who owed the most. And so it is, those the Christ forgives the most sins are those who love him the most. In verse 47, Christ acknowledged that her sins were many, but they were forgiven, for she loved much. Those who are forgiven little love little. Showing love to others covers iniquity. Love washes away sins. When it comes to sinning, we are equals. Let us remember—love can change anything.

The Woman with the Issue of Blood

Luke 8:43-48 mentions a woman who had an issue of blood. After she had exhausted all her money for physicians, she heard of a prophet coming to town. She knew this was her chance of getting healed. Her faith did not question why or how. Her hour had come for a healing. She had to touch the prophet somehow. She was lucky enough to get close to Him and touch the border of His garment. Immediately, after all those years of not being healed, her blood flow stopped at once. Christ turned around and asked, "Who touched me?" The disciples replied, "Master, in this crowd, you ask who touched you?" Christ said, "Strength has gone out of me." The woman fell down before Him with tears in her eyes and said, "It was I who touched your garment." He answered (in verse 48) that she should be of good comfort and that her faith had made her whole, and he told her to go in peace. Let this statement of our Lord Jesus Christ be our guide so that faith and peace will prevail within us in this generation. Let our faith make us whole, knowing that faith can move mountains.

Mary Magdalene

Mary Magdalene is mentioned in several places. Many books have been written about her. Some have stirred up much controversy about her life. It has been revealed that all women come out of the lineage of either Mary, the mother of Christ, or Mary Magdalene, who was called a disciple of Christ. What kind of woman was she? We know she belonged to the inner circle of Christ, and it is believed she was instrumental in organizing the daily tasks of the women in the ministry. We also know that before her ministry work, she was a sinner, because seven demons were told to leave her soul. She was a tormented woman before she met Jesus Christ, but because of her miraculous healing, she followed and served Him. Mary Magdalene believed in the work of God. She used her money and time to devote to His ministry. Because of her devotion and work, her name is mentioned in the Scriptures, and she has become a mystery woman to many in our time.

She Was the First at the Tomb

Mary Magdalene was the first person to arrive at the tomb of Christ at dawn on that Sunday. She found the tomb empty and was perplexed. During the past few days, she had seen more things and witnessed more events than she ever imagined to experience in a lifetime. Mary Magdalene ran and told Simon Peter and another disciple, who returned to the tomb and found it empty. They departed in fear, went home, locked the door, and remained in hiding. Mary Magdalene went to the grave a second time and was surprised to find two men dressed in white. One was sitting at the head, the other at the foot where the body of Jesus had been laid. They asked her, "Woman, why weepest thou?" She wondered if they did not know. She answered, "Because they have taken away my LORD, and I know not where they have laid him." As she walked away, she met a man she thought to be the gardener. Something didn't seem right. She asked him the whereabouts of the LORD's body, for she was ready to move Him to another place. The gardener turned around and said to her, "Mary." She immediately recognized the voice of her LORD and replied, "Rabboni." She took quick steps toward Him, but He cautioned her, "Touch me not, for I am not yet ascended to my Father. But go tell the brethren, and say unto them, 'I ascend unto my Father, and your Father; and to my God and your God'" (John 20:17-18).

Mary Magdalene went to the disciples who were still in hiding to inform them of her physical encounter with the Master. Christ appeared to the disciples and wished them peace. It is said that God reveals Himself to those He loves. The famous writer St. Augustine wrote that the Holy Spirit proclaimed Mary Magdalene as the apostle of apostles! Here we can see and understand the equality of discipleship in the kingdom of God. In the new dispensation, women will be very faithful to God and will be anxious to work for Him.

> Every wise woman buildeth her house; but the foolish plucketh it down with her hands.
>
> Proverbs 14:1

Women Are Saints

> The LORD has made all things for himself: yea, even the wicked for the day of evil.
>
> Proverbs 16:4

Christian Saints

There have always been saints on earth. They are mentioned as far back as there are records and as current as yesterday. There are interesting facts and, in some cases, colorful settings. Many of the saints of old have a liturgical feast celebrated by some churches on certain days. The legends of the saints tell about their daily lives and their sayings and writings. Following are some descriptions of saints' lives whose stories are familiar to us and to whom some people pray. Their lives and circumstances have been very different from ours. The Creator gave them special inspirations. The time has come when it is not necessary anymore to go through intercessors with our petitions, but we go directly to the throne of our Father.

Saint Gertrude

Gertrude's parents and birthplace are unknown. Her parents brought her to the Cistercian abbey in Helfta, near Eileen (Saxony), at the age of five. The sisters who taught her recognized her quick memory and intelligence. She studied Latin and liberal arts. Gertrude had a sparkling character and was very competent but very philosophical. The LORD gave her a vision regarding this, and from that day on, she had only one book in her hands—the Holy Scripture. Countless other visions followed, which inspired the book *Conversion*. From then on, her life was about heavenly communications. Gertrude's mystic work is highly esteemed; some of her revelations are contained in the book *The Herald of Divine Love*. God revealed Himself to her. She spoke to Him, and He, in return, gave her great insight into mysteries. She had the gift of being able to move hearts. Her words were very penetrating and could compel people to think of nothing but God. She was able to lift up downcast souls, and those already on fire were inspired even more. Gertrude died at the age of forty-five. She handled her joys as well as her sufferings with gratitude and humility. She said the greatest miracle is that planet earth was compelled to bear a sinner like her.

Saint Monika

Monika is the patron saint of wives. She was born in Tagaste, in today's Algeria, close to Constantine. Her parents raised Monika as a Christian. Her father made her marry a pagan named Patricius, who was much older than she was and had a violent temper. Her mother-in-law, who lived in the same house, caused many problems for her. Monika turned to prayers and daily church attendance. She bore three children. One was the future St. Augustine, an eminent theologian. Augustine was her pride and joy because he achieved great success in his studies.

Her mother-in-law was heard to say to Monika, "If you can master your tongue, perhaps you can make your husband a better man." Through her patience and long-suffering, she converted her husband to Christianity in the year 370. He died soon after. Monika went to Italy where Augustine lived at the time and with the help of the future St. Ambrose, her son accepted the faith in 386. He accepted baptism the same year as his son, after which Monika declared that all her hopes were fulfilled. She and her son were planning a return trip to Africa when Monika suddenly died at the age of fifty-six. Her son continued in the faith and became the bishop of Hippo. He is widely known for his books *Confessions* and *The City of God* and is regarded as one of the great doctors of Christianity. Augustine died during the fall of the Roman Empire in 430, as the vandals moved into Hippo.

Saint Paula

Paula became the patron saint of widows. She was married to a Roman senator named Toxotius and was widowed at age thirty-five. After she lost her husband and oldest son, she had to raise her other five children by herself. She suffered grievously and gave herself completely over to God. She was one of the women taught by St. Jerome. He urged Paula to leave everything and follow him to Bethlehem. Estochium, her daughter, went with her on the pilgrimage to the Holy Land. In 386, Paula became a leader to some women and was the moving force in building a convent as well as a hospice for pilgrims. She was seen in the streets giving alms to the poor, and she worked to sustain both herself and the poor. Her charitable gifts were extravagant. She took care of St. Jerome's ministry and welfare. Later on, he wrote her biography. She died in Bethlehem at the age of fifty-six, with her daughter, Estochium, by her side. She was buried beneath the Church of the Nativity. Her life was one of servitude to God and humans.

Saint Brigitta

Brigitta, also known as Bridget of Sweden, the patron saint of healers, was born in 1302, the seventh child of a Swedish nobleman named Birger and his wife, Sigrid. During her birth, a priest had a vision from the mother of Jesus, who said, "A girl is born to the Birgers. Her voice will be heard all over the world."

Brigitta's mother died when she was five years old. Her aunt Katharina then took good care of her. By the time she was eight years old, she started to have visions. She was a serious child who listened carefully to the voice within. Her father married her off very young to a prince named Ulf Gudmarrson. They had eight children. Brigitta and her husband were summoned by Queen Blanche and her husband King Magnus II of Sweden to work in their residence in Stockholm, where Brigitta became a lady-in-waiting in 1333. Brigitta had many visions during this time but was ridiculed by the people of the court. She and her husband left the palace in 1339. They promised each other to serve God full time and stay celibate. After a pilgrimage to the grave of St. Jakob, her husband decided to join the monastery of Alvastran in Sweden where he died four years later.

Brigitta gave everything she had to the poor, said good-bye to her children, and entered a Cistercian monastery. Two years later, she founded, with the help of King Magnus a monastery at Wadstena that later became the center of the Brigittine order. Brigitta lived a life of fasting and prayer. In 1349, she traveled to Rome with her daughter Kathariana, and was devastated by the local circumstances. Katharina is also venerated as a saint. During the years 1348 through 1349, the black plague killed many people in Europe. Brigitta worked among the sick in Rome and cared for the poor and the needy. This work made her the patron saint of healers. Before she died, she called her children to her bedside to say good-bye. Her last words were, "Into your hands I order my spirit." She died in 1373 in Rome. In 1374, her daughter, Katharina, took her body to the monastery that Brigitta had founded in Wadstena.

Saint Isabel of France

Isabel of France was born around 1225, as the daughter of Louis VIII and Blanche of Castile. To her mother's surprise, she showed self-control and a love for prayers early on. She studied the Holy Scriptures with intensity, acquired a perfect knowledge of Latin, and added natural history, medicine, and Eastern languages to her studies. In her youth, the young princess fell very ill as a result of mortifications, to the point where her life was in danger. A visionary was brought to her bedside who foretold that she would recover but would give her life entirely to God's service. At an early age, she was promised to the son of the Count of Angouleme, but she broke the betrothal, and her brother, the future St. Louis, had to pay a handsome amount of restitution to the intended groom. Frederick II asked for Isabel's hand in marriage to his son, who was the heir to the empire. But again, Isabel declined, saying that she preferred to be the least in the ranks of the LORD's virgins instead of being the greatest empress in the world. In 1228, she founded the Abbey of Longchamp on the bank of the river Seine. She was often sick and suffered innumerable pain. At the age of forty-six, she died, on a bed of straw.

Saint Teresa of Avilla

Teresa was born in 1515 into the noble family of Alonzo Sanchez de Cepeda in Avilla, Spain. At the age of seven, she ran away to join the Moors, hoping they would kill her so that she would die as a martyr. Those aspirations did not come to pass, and she started reading novels, was flirtatious, and engaged in frivolous chatter. Teresa was twelve years old when her mother passed away. However, at age sixteen, she joined an Augustinus convent in her town. After a pious conversation with an uncle, she became a nun and took her vows in 1534. She delighted in prayers but also loved to carry on secular conversations. She became very unhappy and understood that God wanted all of her. In 1562, Teresa reformed the Carmelite order. St. John of the Cross and Father Jerome Gratian helped her to extend her reforms to all the Carmelite orders. She built austere convents in Avilla, Toledo, Valladolid, Salamanca, and Alba. Her gallant spirit put everybody at ease. She experienced supernatural occurrences. She died during the night of October 4, 1582, attended by Anna of St. Bartholomew. Teresa is one of the most revered saints. She is well known and highly admired by women; her writings are inspiring to this day.

Saint Bernadette

Bernadette was born in Lourdes, France, in 1844, as the oldest of six children. Bernadette was an ailing and undersized child who also suffered from asthma. At the age of twelve, she had to work as a servant. After she celebrated her first communion, she started to have visions from the Virgin Mary—eighteen in all. She was instructed in many things, including that a shrine should be built by the forgotten spring. The Basilica in Lourdes is today a well-known meeting place from where many healings have been reported, and it attracts pilgrims from all over the world.

Because of her visions, officials of the church and the state interrogated her, which caused her great suffering, but she never lost her patience or dignity. In 1866, she joined the motherhouse in Nevers. She was ailing and often bedridden. Her superiors treated her with sarcasm and humiliated her, which she suffered with courage and patience. She said that the role of being ill was her plight. She died in 1879, at the age of thirty-five, in Nevers. During her last night, she was heard saying, "Holy Mother of God, pray for me a poor sinner, poor sinner." Bernadette showed great faith in all of her illnesses.

Saint Theresa of The Child of Jesus

Theresa was born in Normandy on January 2, 1873, to Louis Martin and Zelie Guerin, who were a merchant family that embraced their religion. They had nine children, but only five girls survived; all became nuns. Theresa was four years old when her mother died. She was the youngest of the five girls and showed amazing spiritual knowledge. At two years of age, she was already praying. By the time she was five years old, she understood sermons. She received a prophetic vision about her father's illness to which he later succumbed. The Benedictines of Lisieux brought up Theresa. During that time, she suffered from a strange malady, characterized by violent cries, extended delirium, and fainting spells. In 1888, she entered the convent of the Carmelites. Before she took her vows, she declared that she came to Carmel to save souls and pray for priests. She adorned the chapel with her own paintings and composed songs. Theresa's life was filled with suffering, which she carried with great courage. In 1894, she started to write her autobiography *The Story of the Soul,* which spread all over the world. Two years later she became very ill, which started a spiritual martyrdom for her when the light of faith and the sweetness of hope declined in her. Before she died, she had written, "I want to spend my heaven doing good on earth." In 1897, she died after someone heard her murmur, "I would not suffer less. I love thee, my God."

Mother Teresa

Mother Teresa's name was Agnes Gonxha Bojaxhia. She was the youngest of three children, born in Skopje, Macedonia, in 1910. At the age of seventeen, she responded to her first call to become a Catholic missionary nun. She joined an Irish order, the sisters of Loreto, known for their work in India, and took the name Teresa. Sister Teresa was soon working in Calcutta in India, where she taught geography and catechism at St. Mary's High School. She became its principal. She contracted tuberculosis and was sent away for rest and recuperation. On the train ride to Darjeeling, she received her second call from God. She was to leave the convent and work with the poor on a lifelong assignment from God. How could she walk away?

In 1948, the Vatican granted her permission to leave the Sisters of Loreto to follow her calling from God. She started a school in a slum area to teach the poor. She also acquired basic medical knowledge and treated the sick. Some of her former pupils joined her. The group rented a room in order to be able to care for the homeless who were condemned to die in the gutters. By 1950, the group was called the Missionaries of Charity, and she became known as Mother Teresa, who helped the downtrodden people of India.

She followed in the footsteps of our LORD Jesus Christ, who said, "What you do to the least of my brethren, you do to me."

> A prayer by Mother Teresa for the poor:
>
> "Make us worthy, LORD, to serve those people throughout the world who live and die in poverty and hunger. Give them through our

> hands this day their daily bread, and by our understanding love. Give them peace and joy."

Pope John Paul II said, "Mother Teresa marked the history of our century with courage. She served all human beings by promoting their dignity and respect and made those who had been defeated by life feel the tenderness of God." Former German Chancellor Helmut Kohl stated, "She helped the poorest of the poor, gave them courage to live and the feeling of their worth. Mother Teresa will remain unforgotten and is an example even after her death."

We Are All Saints

Our time also has saints. There are saints all around us. Who is to say we are not saints? We all carry our crosses. Whether devout or agnostic, we all have souls. That spiritual connection runs through every human being. It is the part in us that searches for meaning in life. What matters to us? Do we love one another and help the rest of the world? How do we embrace death? Have we learned from our personal experiences? The answers come from within us. No other person can answer these questions. Our souls speak the truth at all times. Our intimacy with our soul is that sacred place in us that no one can touch. We already have our definition about life, love, community, and the world in us. Once we listen to the voice within and do the will of God, we are saints. In the evolution of mankind, we are on dissimilar spiritual levels, like in school, where different grades have different lessons. Many of us are silent heroes, doing God's work quietly and peacefully somewhere in the world.

Many questions arise: Who is this God we believe in? What words should be used in a prayer? Or should we speak to Him as we have done in childhood? We believed that our God is far away from us, somewhere over the clouds. Now we know that He is in and around us. We are growing up. Should we have different conversations with Him? In our fearful and heartbreaking moments, we cry out to our Father. Let not the transcendent moments in our time of Spirit be but a few, but let them become part of our lives. We all seem to experience dreams, visions, and mysteries. Let us reflect upon them. We should also reflect upon our Father God. Is He sorrowful that He created the world? Does He cry for us when we suffer because of sin? Can we hear Him talk to us every day? The frailty of our communications with God is the human experience.

Once we build into our lives silence and quiet times with God our Father, we will hear His voice clearly. Or He might give us signs along the way. We will talk about the health and growth of our soul. We have to make time for our soul. Time is a rare commodity in our society. After praying and asking God questions, we need to be silent in order to hear His voice. Silence is important when talking to our Father. This wisdom is taught in all religions.

Women Have Only Just Begun

My grace is sufficient for thee, for my strength is made perfect in weakness.

2 Corinthians 12:9

Today's Women Will Come Together

Today's women will come together to understand and comfort each other. We all have a lot in common to validate each other's experiences. The Spirit is with each and every one of us, just like it was in the days of our Savior's mother. Mary Magdalene brought a powerful example to the role of women. In the new millennium, we will adapt her style. In Christ's time, she defined the role of women who can be great servants of God.

We now look for the new role women will play on the stage of life with the guidance of the Holy Spirit. We are a new generation of modern women who bring a new passion and dynamic to the work of God. This holds true as long as we stay humble and trust our Father unconditionally. His obedient children are always willing to do His work.

The Bible's focus is mostly on what God accomplished through the work of men. About three thousand people from Adam to the apostles are named, with fewer than ten percent of them women. Of course, women were always there, from Eve until today. Now that the door has opened, women will step forward and accomplish what was written about us. Christ told us "Greater works will you do, for I will go to the Father." Women are inspired from all over the world and from every faith and will be united in the new kingdom of God. We will be a powerful force. Divided we fall, united we stand strong. We will not scatter, but gather together.

Women Have Only Just Begun

Today we recognize and value the work of Sarah, Rebekah, Rachel, Miriam, and Mary Magdalene. The best is yet to come. Women have only just begun. It was Mary Magdalene who was not identified with a husband. She stood alone and accomplished her ministry work powerfully. She was a person of strength and character. In that era, women were only mentioned in conjunction with their husbands, fathers, or brothers. When the male disciples fled, Mary Magdalene stood by the Christ during His crucifixion and resurrection. We are only told that she was a sinner who was forgiven, which is the same with us. She has deepened our faith and our belief in the work of women. In today's world, we need not be identified with a male. It is God who has guided women into this new role. Through Mary Magdalene, we step out in faith and rediscover the work of God. We are inspired through her to be unafraid to speak up and be heard.

The misconception that Eve gave Adam an apple, which was never stated in the Bible, is now cleared up in the age of the Spirit. Through Eve and Adam, we lost the kingdom of God, which we regain in this time.

The Bravery of Women

In different cultures, men have ruled and still rule over women to this day. Through the coming of the Comforter, which is the Holy Spirit, John 14:26 tells us, "He will teach us all things and bring to our consciousness what we have forgotten." Through this statement, we realize that we do not know all things. The bravery of women has often been overlooked. In the book of Joshua, it was the prostitute Rahab who helped Joshua conquer Jericho by hiding his spies in her house. In the book of Judges, we find Deborah, a prophetess, who called on general Barak to lead an army into battle. He did not want to go without her, so she went with him. She even predicted that only a woman would capture the enemy leader Sisera, which came to pass.

Judith, a widow, dressed in her very best and entered the enemy tent because the Jewish leadership wanted to surrender to the enemy. She went to change the mind of General Holofernes. He became infatuated with her and planned to seduce her. While in the chambers, she decapitated him and took his head. The army fled after that sight.

Women Have Waited Patiently For Their Liberation

Our biblical sisters had to wait many thousands of years for their liberation to finally be heard because it was never the right time for them. We cannot say that those women of ancient times were weak or passive. They were not allowed to step forward and were bypassed. They were either ignored or just viewed as not important enough.

In the ancient texts, women were not mentioned at all, but from the stories of the Bible, we know they did what had to be done. Their endurance prevailed, and they made sure their mission would be accomplished. They were entrusted by God to complete their assignments, from Eve to the woman clothed with the sun and the crown of twelve stars on her head in Revelation 12:1. These women will comfort us, and we will fulfill our destiny on the stage of life. They were willing players and will never leave our hearts. They live on in our spirits in the ever-moving and unfolding spiritual drama that is played out in front of our eyes on this planet that is called Earth.

Women are victorious.

Women Are Becoming Leaders

> Favor is deceitful and beauty is vain: but a woman that feareth the LORD, she shall be praised.
>
> Proverbs 31:30

In The Days to Come

Christ came so that we could follow in His footsteps, which is the ultimate aim for mankind. All differences between men and women are over because there is neither male nor female in the Spirit, for we are all one in Christ Jesus. With the completion of the work of the Holy Spirit, women are taking their rightful places as equals in all things. St. Paul specifically said "male and female," rather than man and woman, to eliminate the aspect of superiority based on sex. With this, the roots of sexual discrimination are eliminated. He said in 1 Corinthians 11:11, "Nevertheless, in the LORD neither is the man independent of the woman, neither the woman independent of the man." 1 Corinthians 12:28 shows God's appointed ones—men and women. The value of the abilities goes equally to the designated person. Whoever fulfills the assignment will get the blessing.

All Positions of Leadership Are Opening

In the era of the Holy Spirit, women will have many positions of leadership. This era started with the new millennium and holds equality for all; old traditions are falling away. A woman can serve God any way she is directed. She can be a preacher, teacher, evangelist, and so on. When the Godhead is upon this earth, He changes the rules, for He said, "Behold, I make all things new," (Revelation 21: 5). He unites the two sexes in holiness. Men and women will walk and talk with God like it was in the garden of Eden before man's fall from grace.

Women Have the Same Power and Gifts of the Spirit

The coming of the Holy Spirit has officially opened the door wide for all women. He has filled them with the same powers and gifts of the Spirit. There is no cause for astonishment or questioning. For God laid down the principle of spiritual matter.

In Christ's Time, Single and Married Women Were Seen With Him

In Christ's time, women walked and talked openly with Him, which was seen by many. The involvement of women was significant at that time in Israel because it went against the Jewish tradition. He conversed with the sinful Samaritan woman who was rejected by her own people, as well as the adulteress caught in the very act by the Pharisees who wanted to stone her. They witnessed the compassion Christ had for women. There were many complaints on this issue, as in Luke 23:2, "We found this man perverting our nation."

Christ gave everyone a clear picture of the rights of women. They were able to share His ministry, to listen to the words of God, to approach Him, and to speak to Him. The mother of the two Zebedee brothers rushed forward as Christ walked the streets and knelt before Him. She begged Him to let her two sons sit with Him in His kingdom—one on His right, and the other on His left side. Christ answered with a statement that is also a teaching for our time and to be taken to heart. He said, "To sit on my right hand, and on my left, is not mine to give, but it shall be given to them for whom it is prepared by my Father" (Matthew 20:20-23).

This tells us that heavenly positions are up to the Father. Our LORD Jesus Christ does not have authority in this matter. He openly prayed to the Father in and for all things. We are to do the same when following in His footsteps.

His ways do not constitute a stumbling block for anyone. Christ had a purity about Him that was radiant. Now the law of love will be accepted in every country in the world, no matter where one comes from, no matter what human laws one goes by. Even though Christ opened the way for women, it took another two thousand years for its fulfillment. Women do not have to embark on a campaign to defend their positions any more. This will come as natural as a tree bearing fruit.

At The Beginning, Woman Was Made From Man. Therefore, Man Must Be Born Of A Woman.

The source of all life is God. For that reason, priority is not given to one sex over the other, for true life is in the union of the two. Man and woman united through God is a perfect human being. God has created us for Himself. Men and women in the future will attain purity of vision and thought. The Holy Spirit in this new dispensation does not eliminate the beauty of His first creation but removes the pitfalls that brought the downfall of mankind. He restores everything in our time to its original perfection.

Men and woman will reject their former behaviors of division and egocentricity, of vain desires and corruption. They will experience the true renewal of spirit and mind as new beings. The new men and new women are in the likeness of God; they will walk in righteousness and will regain the image of our Creator (Ephesians 4:24). They will be changed from corruptibility to incorruptibility. However, this does not change or eliminate the natural distinction between bodies or biological functions. There are no more restrictions, especially in the new kingdom.

A Woman Bore the Christ

Two thousand years ago, our Lord Jesus Christ did not appoint women amongst the twelve apostles, yet it was a woman who bore Him. Mary, the mother of Jesus, would have many important and beneficial things to tell us concerning His birth. However, direct statements or recordings are not given to us.

Throughout the gospel story, women played an important role, whether it was in Bethlehem, Canaan, Galilee, at Jacob's well, in Bethany, Jerusalem, at the tomb, or the upper room. The women followers of Christ served Him in every way they could. Many women provided out of their own means (Luke 8:1-3). During that time, women had to take into account the rules of the Pharisees and other religious groups.

God's strength is made perfect in weakness. Somehow, those women knew that a time would come where they would no longer be subject to human suffering. Christ gave them wings. They had stood in the shadows for too long. Spiritually, their lives took on new dimensions after the death of their Savior. They remembered His words, "The kingdom of God is at hand." Now the kingdom is in our time given to the most sinful generation on earth.

God gives us different gifts, which are equally important. They can be prophecy, service, teaching, healing, and the like (Romans 12:6-7). Phoebe, a deaconess, is an example of a woman appointed in the church. There were many women at that time that made a name for themselves working in the Father's vineyard.

Paul described his workers—Phoebe, a deaconess; Timothy, a fellow worker; Titus, a partner; Prisca and Aquila, fellow workers; Epaphroditus, a brother; Persis, a hard worker for the LORD. Paul was deeply moved by the hard work of women. There were many women who prophesied in the churches at that time. Acts 21:9 tells about the four virgins, the daughters of Philip the Evangelist, who prophesied and shared their gifts with the people.

The Age of Spirit

> Beloved, let us love one another: for love is of God; and everyone that loveth is born of God, and knoweth God.
>
> 1 John 4:7

The Father Awakens Our Souls

Know that there is limitless love available to all life. Blessings come in a myriad of ways. With heartfelt gratefulness, we receive God's grace, which is given without conditions or interruptions. This love keeps giving; there is nothing that we have to earn. It is akin to our earthly father who loves us; we don't have to earn his love. How much more does our heavenly Father love us? Accept it and see the transforming power that works wonders in our lives. God's unending supply is ours to use with joy and gratitude. Awaken to new insights as the light of God guides us through each and every circumstance.

We will be much more intimate with our Father once He awakens our souls. He said, "You have not chosen me, but I have chosen you." The liberation of souls is His goal, and it will take away loneliness, hopelessness, and any form of despair or fear. Separation and isolation will be no more. We will no longer think in terms of limitations.

Let Us Carry Our Cross to the End

My Spiritual Mother, who also came out of conditions of restrictions and limitations, shares with us that we must never forget the profound importance of carrying our cross to the end. If we are lucky to be given the chance to enter into the kingdom of God, which is now here on earth, we will realize the incredible difference between carrying our cross in sin (in this world) or in righteousness (in the kingdom).

If we carry our cross with resentment, anger, fear, or in denial, we should ask the Holy Spirit to help us carry our cross in joy, peace, hope, patience, and tolerance. It is only the Holy Spirit who will give us the ability to carry the cross in love. Which choice do we prefer? We are all carrying crosses.

The Small Voice within Us

Let us awaken our powers, for our potential is unlimited. We all have a quiet voice within us; some call it conscience, others call it instinct. No human being is born without this voice. It is an intuitive guide who leads us aright in life. When that voice speaks to us or gives us an impression, a feeling, or a knowing, we must listen. If we ignore this voice, we grieve the Holy Spirit. We then take a path not assigned for us, consequently we must return to the original road destined for us. We have been taught to ignore this voice and to listen to mass consciousness. Now we must relearn to recognize that voice which speaks to us at all times. This gift is within and available to every human being. We all struggle sometimes with a decision, unsure of what to do. But once we let it go and release the problem to prayer, the answer comes and spiritual insight is given to us. Once we comprehend that God's wisdom is unlimited and our source and inspiration is in Him, we cannot go wrong. Trusting God is a great gift from Him, and it will lead us out of darkness and indecision. He is our compass to find the true way. Our words and actions need to be guided by Him. Our thoughts and decisions must be coming from Him. When change comes into our lives, we grow fearful and alarmed. But even that is from Him and helps us grow. Let us not become anxious or try to avoid that change. He is with us, and He will guide us in all our moves.

> The Lord will guide you continually.
>
> Isaiah 58:11

There Are No Chance Encounters

Each of us has the same measure of power within. It is up to us to reach for this power during our joyous or painful journey through life. Let us listen to the voice within. Signs can be found along the way, which we need to recognize. When we pay close attention, we will find them. There are no chance encounters. Mysterious encounters are taking us to new discoveries in our activities, which lead our souls to grow mightily. Our routes are planned for us so that we do not go wrong. When the student wants to learn, the teacher appears. It may be through a book, someone we meet "unexpectedly," a bumper sticker, a child's laughter, an animal, or something or someone who touches us. Our guide is there to help us every step of the way. Angels are sent our way to help us so that no stone will trip us. If we listen to the voice within, we will no longer be blind and stumble through one crisis after another, constantly falling into traps of our own making, trusting the wrong people, and being lead onto wrong paths.

Once we follow our internal guide, we will find doors opening to new possibilities. New routes are taken as the path unfolds before us. Love will re-enter our lives. Before we can love others, we must first learn to love ourselves, and then we can be at our best. The intimacy with our Father, the voice within, is not a separation of spirit and body. It means being one with Him at all times. We can improve our lives by learning the spiritual laws. We continually make plans for our lives. Our ambitions preoccupy our minds. However,

God is the master-planer. A German phrase states, "*Der Mensch denkt und Gott lenkt,*" meaning, "Humans think, and God guides."

Keep Your Focus in the Present

Our ambitions preoccupy our mind, yet it is said in Psalms 1, "Our delight is in the LORD and we meditate on His law day and night." We should stay in the present moment because we own it. The past cannot be changed, the future is but a promise, only this moment is ours to be fully enjoyed. While we engage in daily activities, our minds may drift at times to things in the past or what might happen in the future. Let us honor the past and believe in our future, but our present moment is enhanced when our attention is with God. Like the sun spreads across the morning sky, so will the joy of God spread in our hearts once we give everything over to Him. Through this wonderful gladness of our souls, we will see goodness in all people. We may not understand their actions, but we will be able to love them anyway.

Old Habits Will Fall Away

We put so much effort into worldly things, even though we know they will pass away. Studying spiritual laws will bring high dividends. When we build a house, we first consider the cost. We do not want to start building and then realize that we cannot finish the project;

so it is with our heavenly mansion. We want to build a strong foundation of faith, a structure that cannot be destroyed, with windows that allow views in all directions, with solid doors, and with a protective roof for all kinds of weather. Old routines and habits will fall away. In the silence of our hearts, we will have long conversations with our Father. He will reveal all things to us and show us things to come. He has a master plan for us. Not only is He a great advisor, He is the supplier of all things.

> "For I know the plans I have for you," declares the LORD, "plans to prosper you and not harm you, plans to give you hope and a future."
>
> Jeremiah 29:11

The Adolescence of the Soul Is Over

The place we find ourselves at this time is not chosen or caused by us. It is a step on the ladder of our growth. Let us not judge ourselves, but let us look at ourselves with open eyes. Thus far, we have been teenagers—checking things out, testing our abilities, running from one place to another, and enjoying ourselves. Now we have to grow up. The soul is ready. Our spirits reveal to us that the soul is waiting. The adolescence is over. The time for silly games has passed. We are now willing to reach for great advancements for our souls. Even physically, we have grown to new heights. We are aware that our bodies must be treated properly. The right food must be eaten or sickness develops. In the past, we have neglected our bodies, which are the vehicles of our souls.

The Body Is a Mystery

Our bodies are mysterious universes, with rivers of blood, different systems, and its own life. When only a small part in our body does not work correctly, we are not whole and we do not feel well. In this new time of Spirit, we realize that our body is an instrument that must be tuned to perfection for the new age and the new condition that we are going into. Our hearts will convince us of this. Once renewed, we will become vegetarians. Our spirits will rise to the occasion, for we are fearfully and wonderfully made. Each cell in our bodies will be changed. A new energy will lift us to new heights. The fears of yesterday will be gone. This change will have many challenges.

In this new time, we will discover for ourselves that partaking of the flesh of animals transgresses totally against the law of love. Were we not told in the Scriptures that man was to be superintendent of all life forms (including animals) that shared common life with him? When sin (disobedience) was introduced into our race, this truth was quite successfully hidden from us with devastating consequences. Yes, in the age of enlightenment, all will embrace vegetarianism.

A Child Does Not Think Of the Future

In the past, we used logic; we reasoned things out. Our beliefs were measured by what we heard or learned. Now we use the inner voice to guide us every step of the way. We will no longer listen to the mind. We will be liberated from the old thinking. Our thoughts will be in the now, which gives us joy, just like a child who neither thinks of the future, nor dwells in the past. A child's joy is in the now. For him it is so easy. However, it is hard for us to be like a child again.

We must free ourselves from the dominance of the mind. The mind likes to return to the past. It repeats itself over and over like an old recording. It loves to repeat negative thoughts. Let us break those habits. We are the masters of our minds, and as such, we can stop any unwanted thoughts. We can retrain our mind not to give us negative thoughts. We can tell our mind, "Are you with me or against me? If you are with me, I like positive statements or nothing at all." To let the mind run the show means we have not changed. Guiding our thoughts will become second nature and is necessary for our souls' growth. Let us get in touch with ourselves; this is the way of the new age. We want to get to the highest and noblest place within us, which is love. The place where we were in the past is not good enough for us anymore. A true transformation must take hold within us. Nobody else can do this for us. We must achieve it ourselves. Each and every one of us must do the work. Many of us find ourselves in places of shame and guilt and wonder how we got there. We ourselves have created this mindset. The evolution of our souls is our goal. We must take the first step. We must want it, and then we surely will achieve it. We have the power to recreate ourselves.

Every Moment Is a Gift

Our Father gives every moment of our lives to us as a gift. Until we turn completely toward Him, we cannot reach a state of perfection. There is now a new awareness of self that concerns the mind and spirit. Natural foods, clear water, and exercise are new interests.

We have come to realize that what we think and speak is important. We have the power of the spoken word. What we speak is what we are. If we believe that our body is healthy and strong, it is. We have to believe with our hearts, speak the affirmations out loud, and repeat them each day. Once our brain hears this long enough, it will start to heal the body. "I am whole, strong, perfect, harmonious, loving, healthy, joyous, wealthy, and wise," is a phrase our mind should hear from us. Once a message is keyed into our computer, it shows up on the screen exactly as we typed the words. So it is with our mind.

We are living in a world of materialism, yet we seem so troubled. Now mankind is walking into the golden age. We have no other choice; otherwise, our destiny would not be fulfilled. The time is here. The Word of God speaks of this time so clearly. We are moving from mortality to immortality, from corruption to incorruptibility.

More discoveries are made in every field of material wonders and medical breakthroughs. The teachings of spiritual laws are coming our way.

This Is the Age of Spirit

We are in the age of Spirit, yet old traditions seem to hang on. Humans still feel stress, fear, and anxiety. Sicknesses of mind and body plague many. Hospitals and institutions are overflowing. The mental anguish of failure, of not measuring up, brings frustrations of the worst kind. Young people cannot face life and cover up their feelings with drugs and alcohol. The mind is misled with shadowy information. Those things are coming to an end. Light will overtake this darkness. All the education and wisdom of the world cannot help us now. We must follow the law of the Spirit and be one with the source of all life. We are nearing our completion.

A teenager is not yet mature. He or she sees things in a different way. Once maturity is reached, a more settled outlook prevails. At the beginning of the last century, the cry was to have an education. Otherwise, one was nothing. In the seventies, we became physical. Exercise was the craze; changing our faces and bodies to be realigned was the way to be. Now in the age of Spirit, we must beautify our hearts, minds, and souls. The inside, the things we don't see, are important.

One Reaps What One Sows

It does not matter if one knows this law or not; it will touch all of us. Had we understood this law and studied it carefully, many of us would not have sown hatred, malice, being unforgiving, and the like. We would have sown positive attributes like peace, joy, and love for each other and ourselves.

If the body is stressed, then there is no balance in the mind. Once we achieve balance, the living expression of wholeness is in us. This oneness in each of us brings forth a peaceful world, which we all long for, and which rightfully belongs to us. This is nothing more than realizing that we have grown up. St. Paul said in 1 Corinthians 3:2, "I gave you milk, not solid food, for you were not ready for it." He meant we were children, but now as we have grown up, we take heavier food for thought. This is the completion of our lives' goals. We are ready for it; it is the evolution and growth of the human soul.

Let Us Please Our Father

We want to live a noble life, to start a lifestyle that is pleasing to our Father. First, we need to know the laws of the Spirit. This begins with studying, reading, meditating, and also surrounding oneself with people of the same mind. We are always students; our learning is never finished. Through studying with an open mind, things become clearer in our consciousness. Then we learn to practice our lessons and apply them in our daily lives. If one teaching is more difficult than another, we need more time for the difficult one. Examinations are given before a student goes on to the next higher class. Our beliefs need to be examined. Sometimes we believe something to be true, only to find out that it was merely a limited concept. Those divine teachings speed up our rapid transformation. Our teachers on the inside and the outside are always close to us.

If we are motivated to change, we should examine why we want to change. Is it for the approval of others? Is it because we search for power, not having found it in the world so far? Or do we want to be more loving, more compassionate toward others? Then our motivation is pure, and we understand and embrace our own destiny by getting closer to the heart of our Father, whose voice we hear more clearly. We will do His will and rise to wholeness and completeness. Find out the reasons why we want to move forward. Once we become a student, we will advance and then become a practitioner. We must check our experiences and know our motives. Let us live an honest life and become who we were destined to be.

It Is Impossible To Outlaw Love

This spiritual awakening will touch every living soul on planet earth, whether they recognize it or not. We have been on automatic pilot for too long. Feelings and emotions we never experienced will come to the surface. Maturity will unfold and everything will be in divine order.

We are discovering the voice of the Father within us, which has always been there, but which we learned to ignore. It does not matter in what country or in what conditions we live, every one has the voice as a guide within. Our soul's great power is love. Love is the greatest power and is searched for in every country in the world. Nowhere is it against the law of the land. Love is the fulfillment and completion of the different stages our souls have gone through.

The experience of loving all of God's creation is awakening everybody beyond the physical and mental understanding. We are waking up from a nap and transforming into mature spiritual persons. This is happening everywhere in the world, to every living soul.

"I Will Pour My Spirit Upon All Flesh."

What the Spirit God pours upon mankind is *love*. This Spirit does not exclude anybody on planet earth. Let Father's creation come back to His heart.

Let us open our heart

Advice from Our Teacher

> Let thy fountain be blessed: and rejoice with the wife of thy youth.
>
> Proverbs 5:18

As we know, women surrounded Christ during His ministry. As we are set free spiritually in our time, what are the new teachings for women?

My teacher, Olumba O. Obu, said in one of his gospels that men should by now realize that they are only half without women. When the two are joined together, they become an entity. He asks whether we ever have come to understand this wisdom. If all men were assembled together in the whole world, no matter what their deliberations, they could only accomplish half. Wherever men congregate to discuss matters, they cannot come to a full conclusion because they are only operating with partial wisdom. They would not want to cause confusion in their midst when deciding on a matter, yet when only half of the wisdom for an issue is available, where does that lead? Where there is trouble, there can be no peace. It is said one should be neither hot nor cold. Women are cool, while men are hot; but together they are a happy medium. Woman is part of man. God took a part of a man to create a woman. That is why a man's thoughts are concentrated on the woman.

Some women are given to certain men for a reason. We can see that in the case of Pontius Pilate. During the trial of Christ, he asked the people who he should release, Barabbas the murderer or Christ. They cried out with one voice, "We want Jesus." As he walked over to the judgment seat, his wife approached him, saying, "Have nothing to do with that just man, for I have suffered many things in a dream because of him." But the chief priests and elders insisted that Jesus be delivered to them. What would have happened if Pontius Pilate had listened to his wife? She told him to have nothing to do with that good man. He chose not to listen to his wife (Matthew 27:15-26).

Husband, Take Advice from Your Wife

Some men do not listen to their wives. It is the spiritual leader who says that a man who takes advice from his wife will know who means well with him or who brings harm to him. The wife might know these things, whereas the man might be ignorant of these facts. The majority of men are good in getting wealth and material things, but most women know the intricacies of life. It is the wife who protects a man's soul. Man has no idea that his life is in his wife's hands. She is usually the first person who knows what is going on with her man in all situations. She is capable of making a man either rich or poor. Many of man's problems and difficulties, as well as unfortunate events, stem from the fact that he did not ask his wife first for her input into the matter. Once he is in adverse conditions, he may run back to his wife to lament. God always listens to the petitions of a wife. Women have suffered much because men do not treat them as equals.

The Penalty for Mistreating Others Is Severe

No matter how much worldly knowledge a man has acquired from various high institutions where he studied, it is useless if he does not treat his wife and others with honor and respect. God cannot answer a man's prayer if he mistreats his wife and others. God reveals to many wives what goes on in the family through dreams. Yet women are still regarded as insignificant in many situations to this very day.

Everything and everyone created by God has a specific assignment to carry out. It is our duty to investigate our assignments and the purpose for which we were created. Know that men and women have the same Father and God. The opinions of both man and woman must be considered at all times. Do men know what role the women will play in life? Many do not, for they do not regard their women's feelings. He might tell her to hush up, to sit down, to keep quiet, and to follow his orders. Father Olumba says that he hears those things and he sheds tears because of them.

Man should know his wife is his sister and that all are one. God is now uniting all His creation on this globe. If one needs a husband or a wife, one should go first before God so that the right person as partner for one's journey will be revealed.

The Children in the New Kingdom

In the kingdom of God that is now on earth, for which we have prayed in the LORD's Prayer, everybody is equal. Let us look at the children. Do the adults regard them as equals? Are their feelings being considered? In the time of Spirit, we do not spank children; that time is past. Why do we not regard our children as equals? Are they not human beings like us? Do we know where the children come from? Our God is their God and our Father is their Father, but because they are children, we think they have no rights. Do we know their assignments in this world? Have we any idea who they are? Could those children now born into this world be much greater than us?

What are they sent to do that we are not able to do? Therefore, we should join hands with our children and give them our utmost cooperation. Let us never

ever regard our children as small, even if they are only one month old. Even a child in the womb knows more than the woman who carries that child. Let us love and regard our children as we love ourselves. Our children have come to make a difference in the world. Generally, a small child is regarded as a small person. Let us treat our children well, and we will be treated likewise in our life. Do we know that our children are more powerful than we are? We are aware that a new broom sweeps well. Let us not punish ourselves by not treating our children as equals.

The Animals in the New Kingdom

Our teacher says we should have the highest regard for everyone and everything God created. There cannot be a distinction or division among us. Call everyone a brother. Any kingdom divided cannot stand. God is uniting the whole world into one entity. Live in peace with one another. Show patience with evildoers. If we have mercy in our hearts, we will be long suffering with our brethren. We have to learn to coexist with all creation. God is the God of the multitudes. If we treat everybody well, we will have power. The same principle goes for the animals. They were created to serve human beings, for mankind's glory, but humans have decided to wage war against the animals by killing them. For that reason, man has lost his glory. That is why there is no peace between man and animals or between humans. Mankind has been thrown into confusion. Let us pray for ourselves.

Following is a gospel concerning women that Olumba O. Obu gave. His gospels usually start with three Bible verses.

First Bible Lesson: Luke 8:1-3

> "... *And the twelve were with him.*
> *And certain women, which had been healed*
> *Of evil spirits and infirmities, Mary called*
> *Magdalene, out of whom went seven devils,*
> *And Joanna the wife of Chuza, Herod's steward,*
> *And Susanna and many others, which ministered*
> *Unto him of their substance.*"

Second Bible Lesson: 1 Peter 3:7-9

> "Likewise, ye husbands,
> *Dwell with them according to knowledge,*
> *Giving honor unto the wife, as unto the weaker*
> *Vessel, and as being heirs together of the grace*
> *Of life; that your prayers be not hindered.*
> *Finally, be ye all of one mind,*
> *Having compassion one of another,*
> *Love as brethren, be pitiful, be courteous:*
> *Not rendering evil for evil, or railing for railing:*
> *But contrariwise blessing;*
> *Knowing that ye are thereunto called,*
> *That ye should inherit a blessing.*"

Golden Text: Romans 8:18 [Golden Text: Romans 8:18]

> *"For I reckon that the sufferings of this*
> *Present time are not worthy to be compared*
> *With the glory, which shall be revealed in us."*

The texts above discuss the various times when our LORD Jesus Christ came in contact with women. They further analyze the contribution of women to support Christ's mission. Now these texts will assist us to prove that women are not the weaker sex, as alleged. Many empires have risen and fallen, but the contributions of women to the success of such empires cannot be underestimated.-

> Consequently, for the purpose of peace, stability, unity, and equitable distribution of wealth, generally, women should be encouraged to pilot the affairs of their families, states, and nations. This is in line with the basic intent of God for His kingdom in the Brotherhood of the Cross and Star, which is God's Kingdom now on earth. Its major characteristics are equality, justice, fairness, love, oneness, and freedom. These are the distinctive qualities with which the Holy Spirit operates.
>
> Men who disagree with the working of this tenet of the Holy Spirit have ill-treated their wives. For that reason, men have suffered great tribulations. God, who is the controller of destiny, promotes equality. It is totally wrong for

a man to see himself more favored in the sight of God.

A woman is the glory of the man. Similarly, a man is the glory of Christ. However, the creation of woman from man, which forms the basis for women being ill-treated by their male counterparts, is completely invalid and unacceptable. This must be stopped. It is love that prevails.

I am the embodiment of this teaching. My daily life exemplifies this. I exhort the male population to treat women with due respect and decency. For an easy comprehension of this sermon, read the first Bible lesson again.

A wise man loves and cherishes his wife. It is rather surprising that this recondite wisdom eludes most men in the world. Until now, you will notice with amazement that even professional men indulge in the primitive act of ill-treating their wives. Conversely, women should not nag their husbands. Being the glory of her husband, she should radiate peace and love.

As illustrated, women are seen as the source of mundane things. It is desirable that men love their wives so that they may be abundantly blessed. To ensure a problem-free life, men have to lay a proper foundation. That foundation is to love their wives. If men doubt those teachings, it is imperative that they learn and practice them. Only through experience will the truth be confirmed to them. A lot of success and progress are often noticed when women are given equal opportunity to serve God. He has endowed men with power, skill, wisdom, and understanding. To women He gave love, patience, endurance, mercy, humility, meekness, and longsuffering. These gifts do not substitute each other. They rather complement each other. It is therefore important that men and women stay together for an easier life.

Our LORD Jesus Christ and His disciples did not engage in any commercial activities. It was women who supported them. You will note that women were featured prominently during the death and resurrection of Christ. In fact, their contributions were indeed immeasurable. Read the second lesson again.

Any man who complies with those teachings will enjoy peace and progress. It is the function of our God to transform mankind, while Mother God gives material needs. Consequently, one cannot dwell in isolation. Since the spirit cannot operate without the flesh, the flesh also needs the spirit for spiritual benefits. It is imperative that a man cohabits with his wife in love, understanding, and peace. A man and a woman must share equal rights and privileges.

The work of transformation exists in various forms. If your husband is incapacitated, do not lament or weep. You may not know that he is being transformed. Tribulation is like a springboard that leads to eternal life. Consequently, overcoming tribulation is a "sine qua non" to being crowned in this kingdom. If you are falsely accused and even sentenced to imprisonment for no just cause, be exceedingly glad, for your Master, Jesus Christ, suffered greater things than these. When you go the way of the cross, rejoice for you are blessed. Even if you are injured, rejoice again, provided it is for the sake of the kingdom. Do not allow transitory things to cause you to derail from the path of righteousness. One cannot compare the glory of the Christ, living or dead.

Pontius Pilate advised Christ to escape to another country for his safety. His disciples were ready to fight in His defense to set Him free. He did not take the escape route, for He knew His assignment, which was to shed His blood for the salvation of many. If He had run away from it, eternal glory would have eluded Him. The hours of suffering He endured have been transformed into eternal glory.

"Blessed are ye when men shall revile you, and persecute you, and shall say all manner of evil against you falsely for my sake. Rejoice and be exceedingly glad: for great is your reward in heaven." Therefore, do not question any situation, for God knows better than you do. Certain misfortunes that befall mankind are there to call humans back to order. Count everything as a loss for the privilege to enter into this new kingdom. For we suffer, even as Christ has suffered. Face your tribulation with courage and patience.

Thank you, Father Obu.

First, let us thank our teacher for his eternal words. What have we learned from those words? They make many things clear. We know from his words that men and women are equal. He mentioned that women should be encouraged to pilot the affairs of their families, states, and nations. He gave men advice by telling them that even if men should get together to try to solve problems, if the other half is not there, then they will have only half the wisdom. A man who listens to his wife has peace in his life. What great words God gives the world! His words give a new understanding of the relationship between man and woman. It is no wonder that an angel said to God, "Who is men that thou are mindful of him?" God is ever willing to teach mankind. After all, He loves His creation and is mindful of it. He tells us we should count our tribulations as nothing, but be ever mindful to reach the kingdom of God.

Who among us is without problems? Every one carries his or her own cross. He also is very clear on the mistreatment of women. It is a heavy weight a man carries, and he is being told to abstain from such oppression.

In the age of Spirit, those negative behaviors will disappear, for men will be guided by love, not by ego. Their eyes will open and they will acknowledge that they have failed by not accepting women's wisdom. Then women will not wonder anymore why they had unsuccessful and painful unions. Once more, they will be together in love with the men that God put beside them to have a divine marriage. Once a man loves and cherishes his wife, and that union is of the Spirit, the partnership will have power. A woman looks for a man who loves and cherishes her and should settle for nothing less.

The Kingdom of God

> Having made known to us the mystery of his will, according to his good pleasure which he has purposed in himself: that in the dispensation of the fullness of times he might gather together in one all things in Christ, both which are in heaven and which are on earth; even in him.
>
> Ephesians 1:9-10

Since the mysteries of His will are now revealed, it pleases God to bind and gather all things. Even heaven and earth are coming together as one. Needless to say, this includes men and women.

The Kingdom Is Lowered To Earth

Two thousand years after the Christ, the kingdom of God is now lowered to earth. Humans have prayed for this in the LORD's Prayer: "Thy kingdom come." Where is our faith? Where are we standing? He said, "I come like a thief in the night." Are we prepared for God to knock on our door? This is the greatest time to be on earth. We will be witnesses to the incredible changes and their impact on all creation, especially the human race. Through growing awareness, the circle of humanity is coming together as *one*. As we are yet standing in darkness, we can already see the first rays of light. Men and women will be at the forefront to help with the work in the kingdom of God. We will incorporate God's work into our daily lives, just like we incorporate our hobbies. In fact, God's work will become our hobby.

We are walking hand in hand toward a new day. Without realizing it, love has made its way into our hearts. A golden age is emerging, but first we must go through trying times that will test our hearts and souls. Humanity as a whole is searching for answers. Spiritual wisdom is given to those who are ready and willing to receive it.

The spirit world has come to earth in order to help us with this transition. God is now on earth, directing the operation. When the battle is the fiercest, the general goes to the front lines. He is now talking to each and every one of us directly. We do not need intercessors anymore.

The kingdom of God that we prayed for in the LORD's Prayer will intertwine and absorb all worldly kingdoms. Are we ready and willing to work in this new kingdom? Or are we already working in the vineyard of our Father? Either way, this is the greatest time to work for God. Greater is the work in this turbulent time than that of the Apostles—greater than in past times. This new kingdom has a name, which comes from above:

Brotherhood of the Cross and Star

Brotherhood represents all of God's creation. The cross represents humankind, which has gone through trials and the time of the cross. The star is given to us as the prize. In Revelation 22:16, God tells us that He is the bright Morning Star. Brotherhood of the Cross and Star is the new name of the kingdom of God and is to be honored all over the world. No matter what religion we find ourselves in at this time, we are lucky if we find ourselves in this kingdom.

We are standing on the threshold of a new dispensation. We are in the middle of the changeover. The greatest move is upon mankind, from the natural to the supernatural. While we are still limited, soon we will become limitless. Our hope and our eyes are now on the architect of time, for time belongs to Him alone. He is the teacher of the new laws on earth. The old wine is finished and we are now drinking new wine. In this new time, we have to make up our minds as to whom we will serve. We cannot serve two masters, as we have done in the past. We are heirs to a great estate, while the Father calls His children from all over the world. It is said that in brotherhood, all creatures of God take their rightful positions. Brotherhood has existed before the physical universe. The way things are practiced in brotherhood is the way it is practiced on all planes of manifestations. Planet earth is one of the last planets to be brought into the circle of love. We are already members in the new kingdom, for we all belong to the great brotherhood of men.

> Fear not, little flock; for it is your father's good pleasure to give you the kingdom.
>
> Luke 12:32

The Greatest Time to Be On Earth

> Do you not know that your body is the temple of the Holy Spirit which is within you, which you have from God, and that you are not your own?
>
> 1 Corinthians 6:19

Join The Circle of Love by Being the Father's Loving Child

The man and woman in the garden of Eden had all their needs fulfilled, and all things were lavishly given to them. The serpent in the garden of Eden introduced them to good and evil. As Adam and Eve saw duality, they had to leave their consciousness, as well as the garden. All the following generations inherited this condition and the belief in good and evil.

Do we feel separated from God our Father? Go back to that circle of love within you that God extends to all of His creation. To be away from His heart divides us within, as well as without. Humans have created division, sickness, death, limitations, and perversion of every kind, which come from man's perspective of good and evil. With our new hearts, we can only see the good.

Once we are no longer satisfied with only the intellectual and physical existence, we will then search our hearts and minds. The change will come when we are ready, just as a first grader cannot go to high school because he would not understand the teachings. But once we are ready, we will move forward and see our goal. Others will join us on this journey. The time will come when the masses will recognize this wisdom and follow. This search has already started in many hearts with this generation making it its goal. The race is on, and we are on the way to the future.

The Highest Wisdom Is Within Us

We will start communicating with our souls and with our God. Our old thinking will cease. We will rediscover that the transcendent God of old is living within us. This awesome truth will awaken our senses and let us know that truly our bodies are the temple of God. We are His cities, and He dwells with us. The highest wisdom is within us, and His presence is always there. When we feel rejected, jealous, or lack self-esteem, let us talk to our Father within. Then we have instant access to vital and higher wisdom. The Word of God says that He will dwell with us. We will be His people again.

> I heard a great voice out of heaven saying, behold, the tabernacle of God is with men, and he will dwell with them, and they shall be his people, and God himself shall be with them, and be their God.
>
> Revelation 21:3

Women's Rights are At the Forefront

A shift in the way of thinking and values in every category has arrived. Relationships and women's rights have come to the forefront. A commitment to learn about spiritual laws becomes important. There is a general dissatisfaction with the administration of worldly affairs. We are moving slowly away from materialism. Let us look at the new happenings in the world with our hearts, not with our brains.

We can become what we always dreamed of being but thought to be impossible. Now it becomes possible. Together we can take the journey into our unknown spirituality and come to the realization that we have a divine nature. It will take willingness on our part to discover our unlimited potentials. This generation will experience the incredible power of God through the baptism of fire and the Holy Spirit. As the Son of God was the first fruit in His generation, so will we be the first to enter into the kingdom of God in this generation. During this era, we will be catapulted out of our comfort zones.

We Are Searching For Security

The daily television images bring us discomfort. We are looking for security, which seems to have been taken away from us. We are searching for someone who can touch our lives in a significant way. What we don't realize is that this is not to be found on the outside. It is within us; we have to change ourselves, as well as our hearts. A wonderful spiritual awakening is on the horizon. We will look for guidance from the higher power for expanded experiences. Different crises are happening on earth at this time. Some are hazardous, while others are painful; all are full of suffering. Even our environmental, social, and personal worlds are crashing, which compels us to look for a better way to live. Crises change us. They seem to awaken us and make us respond differently.

The state of egotistical, self-centered consciousness is over. Changing from a high technology and a polluting world that destroys itself, to a new world that is life enhancing, loving, and compassionate, is not an easy task. As we utilize modern tools like the internet to interact and communicate with each other and have access to the intelligence of its system, so can our souls interact with our Father—the all-wise, all-powerful, all-present intelligence.

We seem to be slow learners. What worked for us in the past does not work for us anymore. We are the stewards of this planet and responsible for our own future. When we come out of our mothers' wombs, we scream and kick. We are now being reborn into a new life and a new condition. We cannot return to our mothers' wombs.

Are we willing to make this transition? Have we identified ourselves as being willing? Are we ready to join each other on a personal but also on a planetary scale? Ask for this power in this hour and become filled with higher wisdom. We are relearning what we always knew.

> They that be wise shall shine as the brightness of the firmament; and they that turn many to righteousness as the stars for ever and ever.
>
> Daniel 12:3

We Are Stars Forever

Once we turn others to righteousness, we will be stars forever and ever. This is not a new religion. We come from every faith and background, including those who have never heard of God. We become a more spiritually attuned and spirit-centered society. Many went before us—Jesus, Buddha, Krishna, Mohammed, and other great teachers and mystics like St. Frances of Assisi, Julian of Norwich, St. Teresa of Avila, and St. Catherine of Siena, including the more contemporary Padre Pio. They were living in clarity well beyond their ordinary consciousness. They saw the world with different eyes. They were in the world, but not of the world. Some lived behind closed doors and went through anguish and ecstasy to gain access to the spiritual world. Some were able to breath in energy like electricity. Others were divine healers who accomplished their works through love, forgiveness, and faith. If we have not reached higher consciousness, we are not awake yet. None of the ones who went before us ever asked to be returned to ordinary consciousness. They left us with great teachings. They were gifted individuals ahead of their times. They gave us a hint of the coming evolution. God, in His mercy, gave them insights into our future. However, it was not yet the time for the elevation of consciousness of the masses.

People with higher consciousness achieved a state not known to most others. We are the lucky generation that was born at this time to witness the great changes happening at this moment on planet Earth. These elevated teachings will help us through the transformation. We have no choice but to begin this journey and evolve to places where great masters went before us. Few have tread upon this new ground and newfound soil. This journey will be exciting and exhilarating. On this journey of the heart, we will come to realize what the mystics of old have always known that we are divine, connected to the universal intelligence, and we have the abilities to be active participants. Our partnership was established a long time ago, but through the ages and through sin, we lost our contact and forgot that we have, and always had, a connection with the divine.

The True Work Is Starting

As we have entered the third millennium, we begin our true work on this earth. We will realize that we are a world community. We will not say we came from this or that country, but that we are citizens of the world. In the new world and the new life, cosmic consciousness will be the norm. The people of the world will work together in all fields to help planet Earth to sustain us. We will move from our egocentric selves to God-centered people who will be driven by love. Respect for our planet and every kind of life form will be paramount. Never again will one of God's creatures have to die to satisfy our appetites. The inner wisdom that lies within all of us will be our guide.

Mother Earth will restore and heal herself of the pain and pollution we caused her. The old demons will not follow us, for we will be liberated from any kind of bondage. Women will become the missing pieces in the puzzle in the organizing and ruling of the world. Our social systems will be transformed. Our current biological life cycles will be changing, which will lead us to the universal life that was promised to us.

The Masses Are Waking Up From Their Sleep

Are we ready for the evolution of this earth? Millions of us have been waiting for this opportunity to serve a great cause. We might not know yet what is going on, but we have a desire to help. There is no roadmap yet, only a great vision. In other words, the choir is not yet singing, but the singers are being interviewed. Many have spoken in the past to wake up the masses from their sleep. If they were not heard, the time was not ripe. However, they painted us a picture of our future. We all can become creators of a positive world by thinking and doing loving deeds. If women ruled the world, would there be wars? We should never just do nothing. We are ever moving, ever evolving, ever going forward to a greater future.

Great Changes Are Upon Us

An emerging reality is moving the human race to a higher plane. Great changes are upon us. Those changes are not to be feared, but embraced, for they are for our good. The evolution of mankind's spirit and soul is in progress. The alarm clock is ringing to awaken our spiritual and physical consciousness.

This is a challenge as well as an opportunity for the human race. Our planet is making a transition in every way. The new order calls for spiritually motivated people to embrace love again. We love our families and maybe a few relatives and friends. Some have problems with the few people in their lives. Now we are going back to love. This planet called Earth will be ruled by love.

The media speaks of violence, war, and dissent around the world. We do not hear of a reawakening of this planet. We believe that the earth is breaking down instead of having breakthroughs. When we read the newspaper or watch TV, we feel we are nearing the end. The new conditions we are moving into are not newsworthy or are not yet recognized by the media.

A Time of Love, Peace, and Joy

All this happens by design, without many realizing its importance or effect. A time of love, peace, and joy will emerge. It is the Holy Spirit's work to pour His spirit upon all flesh (Acts 2:17). Many, including important people, will look for the Holy Spirit in our time; salvation will be openly searched for. Noted men of the world will wear a white *soutane* and preach the Word of God in the streets. Many will go into the streets to bring this message to the masses. Love will be learned again, like a child is learning to take the first step. We have followed a wrong vision of love. Christ told us in Revelation 2:4-5 that we have left our first love and that we should repent and do the first works, or else He will remove our candlestick out of its place.

The love between a man and a woman is spoken of in every language on earth—in songs, poems, and stories. Yet, this love is conditional. If one of the parties does not do as the other expects, love ends for them.

However, real love never ends. It has no beginning and no end. It touches us every moment of our lives, and we see it in every creation of God. Once we learn to respect all of God's creation, we truly love. Then God will invite us to be in the perfect circle of love that He has with all of His creation. One cannot say that one loves God but hates his brother. This is not possible, for his brother is God's creation, and the Creator loves His creatures. In this time of Spirit, we realize that every being is of God's making, and we love and honor every person coming our way.

The Greatest Time on Planet Earth

This new golden age we are moving into belongs to everybody. It is the greatest time for us to be on planet Earth. We were born at this time for a reason. The spirit world is doing great work on this earth. Heaven and earth are coming together. However, this is not the time to think of more wealth, greater power, more national pride, personal gain, etc. Something much greater is coming. Each and every one will know that to return to the divine within us, the unbroken link with our Father is the goal. This we have known previously but have forgotten. We will return to a life of obedience to the higher will, the voice within us that speaks always to and with us, who is leading us every step of the way.

When Christ was physically on earth two thousand years ago, many were inspired to embrace a new way of thinking. Now another new phase is here, whether we like it or not. Higher consciousness for all is the next stage of our evolution. We are starting to wake up, look around, and see many puzzling occurrences. During the last hundred years, we saw the births of the environmental movement, the human rights movement, the right to life movement, the women's movement, and so on. There are reasons for all of these because the awareness on planet Earth is growing.

Expect the Unexpected

We wonder how all of this will come about. Expect the unexpected, because our Father is guiding us into a new time. For *He* said, "See, I make all things new" (Revelation 21:5). When a house is being torn down to make room for a new one, a lot of dust and debris is created. So it is when old things disappear. When old systems brake down, debris and confusion are created. However, this is for the betterment of this world.

Women of the world, we have a great job to do. Let us begin our work. It was designed for us at this time. Let us walk to the empty tomb of our LORD Jesus Christ to take on our assignments with joy, gladness, and solemn awe, for we have overcome the cross and are now ready to take our crown. The equality of men is a great gift we can give to our children and those who come after us. The empty tomb of the Christ signifies that the human race is acquitted and forgiven. Death has become the gate of life. When the King arrives, He brings the kingdom with Him. He comes with a new name (Revelation 2:17).

The Healing of the Soul

The paradigm shift has begun. Our bodies are being changed on the cellular level.

Our minds, as well as our spirits, are being changed. The great healing in this age of Spirit is not the healing of the body, as wonderful as that may be, but that of the soul. There have always been healings and miracles, which are important to us when we are sick. These have manifested since time immemorial. The healing of the body is not the true miracle of this age. Many have been physically healed but ignored their soul. The healing of the heart and soul is of paramount importance.

The Great Light Has Emerged

We are still living in a world full of darkness, but a great light is emerging. This light will illuminate the whole world, and darkness will disappear. We are happy when everything in our lives goes our way. Once sickness and troubles come, we are distressed. We have to learn that we cannot always stay in bliss. We also have to take the path through the valley of pain and despair to learn life's lessons. We enjoy the view from the top; but where joy is, there is also sorrow. We all would like to always live on the bright side.

Where there is new life there is also death. We all know this, yet most fear death and look at it as an ending. Yet it is just the beginning. Life never ends, because energy cannot be destroyed. It is merely a transformation to another existence. In the age of the Spirit, the fear of death will be gone. Once we learn to love unconditionally, death disappears, for it is part of the old order. Some have been at death's door only to be told to return to earth. Through this, our heavenly Father taught us to understand that there is nothing to fear. From those experiences, we have received divine assurances that life continues. Our own soul also reveals to us that this life on earth is not our real home. We are merely walking on this planet as time travelers.

Afterword: The Baptism of Fire

> The mysteries, which hath been hid from ages and from generations, but now are made manifest to his saints.
>
> Colossians 1:26

Mysteries Were Hidden On Purpose

Mysteries that have been hidden are now revealed to the whole world. Are we ready for those mysteries and willing to accept them?

The Baptism of Fire

This age of the Spirit brings us the baptism of fire. This is important information, which may be accepted or rejected. Let us be guided by our spirit. This is a matter of the Spirit. This baptism leads to spiritual completeness. It is for all of mankind, and it was promised to us from the beginning, to be given at this time. Many will say, "I have been baptized already." This may be true, for most have received the baptism of John the Baptist that is for repentance only. Matthew 3:11-12 states,

> I indeed baptize you with water unto repentance; but he that cometh after me is mightier than I; whose shoes I am not worthy to bear: he shall baptize you with the holy Ghost and fire.

We received the baptism of *repentance*, which was enough in the past. This new baptism speaks of the time of judgment in which we are. This baptism of fire was not available before. We might wonder why our pastors have not told us about it. They have not been and might still not be aware of it. If they had known, they would probably have told us. Once they hear about this soul-saving wisdom, they will take their flocks to be baptized with this baptism into the kingdom of God. All things are then accomplished for mankind. Who gives this special baptism? Whoever has been baptized may baptize others, be they man, woman, or child. One does not have to be a clergy to baptize others, but one needs to be baptized into this kingdom. This baptism is for the *forgiveness* of all our sins. Then one is clean before God. The previous baptism was for the *repentance* of sins; this one is for the *remission* of sins.

The Greatest Gift in Our Time

To receive the Holy Spirit through this baptism is the greatest gift God can give us. Ask for forgiveness of sins and get baptized. This is the fulfillment of all things; then we can hear the voice within us more clearly. This compares to an electrical appliance; once it is connected to the outlet, it works. The true teaching from our Master is the voice within. He said, "The kingdom of God is within." Once His wisdom is integrated into our daily lives, we will follow our first nature, which is the Master in us. The flesh is our second nature, or the slave. So far, we have let the flesh rule us. That time is over. It caused us much pain. We will embrace the new life and the new order. Christ said on the cross, "It is finished." This means the former things have passed away. Two thousand years is but a moment in time. Christ told us,

> Except a man be born again he cannot *see* the kingdom of God.
>
> John 3:3

> Except a man be born of water and of the spirit he cannot *enter* into the kingdom.
>
> John 3:5

Once we are born again, we can *see* the kingdom of God. However, we can only see it and are not there yet. When we are born of water and the Spirit, we then *can enter* into the kingdom. To be born again is the first step, but not the only one. Christ spoke of two steps.

The Great Secret in This Generation

Spiritual secrets are steadily revealed in this generation. The seven seals are opened now (Revelation 5:5). The whole human race will walk freely through this baptism into the kingdom of God. Many of you will say, "I have never heard of this. Can I be baptized?" Pastors and shepherds of the flock, adhere to this new wisdom from above. For Christ said, "I have yet many things to say, but you cannot bear them now." After two thousand years, is this generation ready? The water baptism of John is over. He said, "One mightier than I will come." We know Christ never baptized anyone (John 4:2). He gave us the LORD's Prayer to ask for the kingdom to come. We have arrived at this time. How can we avoid it?

Here is an earthly example to give us a heavenly pearl. This baptism is like a mother bathing the child before daddy comes home from work. She wants the child to be clean for his or her father. So it is with this baptism. When the King arrives, we must be clean before Him. That is why it is given in our time. The King has arrived to set up His kingdom. Once the Father says we are clean, no one can claim otherwise.

John Baptized in the River Jordan

John the Baptist baptized men and women in the river Jordan. He made no distinction between male and female. He exhorted all to repent. The clear plan of God is that women should work side by side with men, may it be physical or spiritual. All humans, women and men, have the right and the responsibility to save their own souls and make the world a better place.

Whatever we do, let us do it in love. We should listen to our hearts. If this baptism is ours, believe, and we will receive it. After the baptism, our life will change. This might happen quickly or slowly. As our spiritual mother said, "We wish not for any of our Father's children to miss the incredible blessings of the spiritual age of the Son of Man."

> The things which are impossible with men are possible with God.
>
> Luke 18:27

Those who have received this baptism will know that the new name of God reigns supreme. This new name is mentioned in the Revelation 2:17: the *O*mnipotent, *O*mnipresent, and *O*mniscient name of God. This new name, O. O. O., is very powerful. We will notice the change in our minds and hearts. Humans will become more aware of their spiritual nature after receiving this baptism and the power of the name that is above all other names. Every cell and every atom in us will respond to this new name.

Prayer

Let thanks and praises be given to our heavenly Father in the name of our LORD Jesus Christ. Amen.

Let dominion and power be given to our heavenly Father in the blood of our LORD Jesus Christ. Amen.

Let majesty and might be given to the Holy Spirit, even now and forever more. Amen.

Holy, holy, holy art thou Almighty Father, maker of heaven and earth.
We, your children, come before you on bended knees and ask for the forgiveness of our sins.
We come from hardship and pain to receive your blessings in this new time. Father, we are ready and willing to forgive those who have

done us wrong, knowing that you are the righteous judge.

Thank you, Father, for bringing your children together in this generation and letting them know that all of your creation is one. Let us take our rightful place in humility and with thankful hearts. Give us the ability to speak your new name and be the peacemakers you intended us to be.

Let thanks and praises be given to you, Almighty Father, in the name of our LORD Jesus Christ. Amen.

Let dominion and power be given to you in the blood of our LORD Jesus Christ. Amen.

Let majesty and might be given to God, even now and forever more. Amen.

Bibliography

Chapter One: *O Magazine*, April 2003, page 177, (Young girl's quote)

Chapter Four: Shopper Newspaper, Debby Wood; "Hot Flashes! Confessions of a Frazzled Floridian."

Chapter Eight: *Book of Saints*, St. Gertrude, St. Monika, St. Paula, St. Brigitta, St. Isabel of France, St. Teresa of Avila, St. Bernadette, Mother Teresa.